TO WHOM SHALL WE GO?

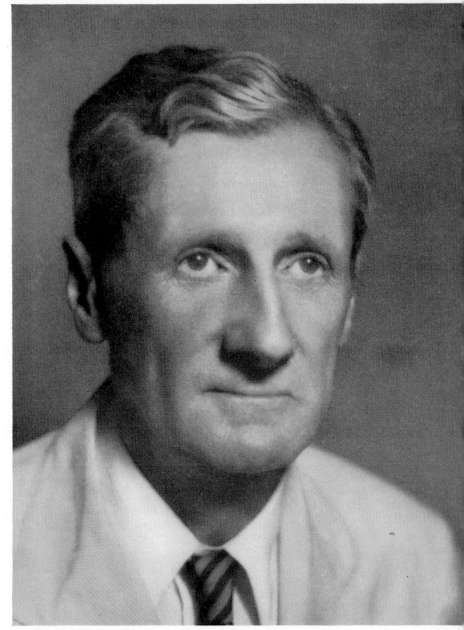

Blackstone Studios, New Y

DONALD MACPHERSON BAILLIE
1887 - 1954

TO WHOM SHALL WE GO?

D. M. BAILLIE

Late Professor of Systematic Theology
The University of St. Andrews

Together with a Biographical Introduction by
JOHN DOW
Professor-Emeritus, Emmanuel College, Toronto

CHARLES SCRIBNER'S SONS

New York

NOTE

NONE of the sermons here printed was written with any thought of publication, though some of them were broadcast. They have been selected from a very large number by a few friends and are now given to a wider public in response to a number of insistent demands. It will be seen that there is no attempt at 'fine writing' in any of them. They are all couched in the language of direct address; for it was this language that was most characteristic of the preacher, and in the pulpit he used none other. They have been printed as they were written. Parts of some may seem to overlap parts of others; but no attempt has been made to eliminate such repetitions, since they may serve to indicate to the indulgent reader the points which the preacher was most anxious to bring home to his various audiences.

CONTENTS

III

SERMONS ON VARIOUS OCCASIONS

MEMOIR

AGAINST the jagged peaks cleaving the skyline, the pine-clad slopes, the blue-green mountain loch, most appropriately he stands, a true son of the Scottish Highlands. It was in Gairloch in Wester Ross that Donald Macpherson Baillie first saw the light of day on 5th November 1887. Idyllic and fairy-like in the blue haze of a summer sun as seen across the narrow strait from Flodigarry in the Isle of Skye, it is really a grim and rugged shoreline breeding a hardy race of crofters and fishermen who have preserved the soft speech and rich folk-lore of the Celt. Hemmed in between the changefulness and terror of the sea and the beauty and majesty of the hills, the Gaels have never lost a sense of the mystery and tragedy of human life, and so to the consolation of religion they have turned with passionate seeking. The tender piety of the ancient Celtic faith lived on and was caught up to the enrichment of the evangelical fervour of the Free Church that swept the northland in 1843. To recapture something of that spiritual background let us go back to Donald Baillie's native parish. In the Gairloch it was the voice of the eloquent Duncan Matheson that reasoned of penitence, faith, and the merit of the one atoning sacrifice. In *Disruption Worthies of the Highlands* Kenneth Macdonald tells how few ministers more impressed their hearers with the holiness of God, the sacredness of His house, the solemnity of His service and the authority of His Word. When a visiting probationer failed to strike the authentic note Matheson coolly stood between preacher and Bible, and commanded him to sit down. It was to this heritage but with his own methods and appeal that the Rev. John Baillie came from Moy and Tomatin in the days of soul-searching Communion Services in the

'Leabaidh'. He was a man who must have had power behind his words, for what he had said in a baptismal sermon was lovingly treasured and repeated fifty years after. It was late in life that John Baillie wooed and won Annie Macpherson and had the joy of welcoming to his household three sons in quick succession. Death claimed him after six years of wedded life, and with fine courage the young widow in the early nineties of last century set out to make a new home in Inverness, where education opened her portals invitingly for the three boys, John, Donald and Peter.

Inverness has beauties in abundance to stir the growing mind, and Donald Baillie ever carried in his affection the swift-flowing Ness, the Black Isle with its banks of yellow broom, the snow cap on distant Ben Wyvis, the lone stretch of Culloden Moor that has sent its dirge down the years. But it was the churches and schools that a wise mother sought out in the Highland capital. Donald always claimed that he did no work at school, but that was belied by his intimate knowledge of Shakespeare, Scott, Dickens, the poets and classics generally. There was a mutual stimulus and emulation in that trio of brothers. We can imagine many a competition for the highest chair to serve as pulpit. 'John,' said Donald one day, 'I'm going to write a book called *Brothers of Famous Men* and, John, the first chapter will be about you!' The Royal Academy is noted for the distinction of its masters—like W. J. Watson—and for the Celtic genius of its students. The discipline of the Academy was touched to higher issues by the inspiration of the Church, then rich in vital personalities, the spiritual home of the Baillie family being the Free North, where Murdo Mackenzie exercised a remarkable ministry. It was no mean city that within a few short years sent out from its gates principals for Princeton and New College, professors for Cambridge and St.

Andrews, preachers for some of the finest Scottish pulpits, and ecumenical leaders for two continents.

Mounting an old Edinburgh tramcar as it lurched its way along Princes Street and headed round the West End, in the winter of 1909, you might have noticed, clad in the inevitable drab mackintosh, a stooping student figure with a face deeply and nobly chiselled and a shy glance of unusual sharpness. Once seated aloft, he has whipped out from his vest pocket a set of calling cards. These he turns rapidly over and over. It is his way of memorising Hebrew words for an approaching examination by Professor J. A. Paterson. And it is the habit of a man who has already mastered the art of filling in the odd moment that you and I can waste in idly gazing round. Donald is now a student of Theology at New College. In Edinburgh University, where his brother had already made Baillie a formidable name, he has had a brilliant career, winning the medals in Moral Philosophy and Metaphysics, both Ordinary and Honours, and George Saintsbury's prize for English Verse; and is soon to add the J. E. Baxter Scholarship and the assistantship to Professor James Seth. He is on his way to Braidburn Crescent, where Mrs Baillie has now established her home while the three sons complete their education at the University. To share an evening of intercourse in that home was the joy of many a student.

The brothers Pringle-Pattison and James Seth, beloved teachers of philosophy, had laid foundations on which the New College professors continued to build: Alexander Martin, master exponent of the Christian ethic, 'than which there can be none higher'; H. R. Mackintosh, already deeply engrossed in his Christological studies, his grave and beautiful eyes often filling with concern over our youthful heresies; H. A. A. Kennedy, vivid and refreshing expositor of the Word; A. R. MacEwen, whose animated utterance literally sprayed us with the lore of the Ancient and the Celtic Church.

3

These were the days when the historical criticism of the Scriptures was producing its fruits and the Jesus of history was the consuming study. The student mind was then enamoured of liberalism, and the custodians of orthodoxy had a hard task to defend the citadel. Enthusiasm was whetted by semesters in Germany. Donald Baillie spent summers in Heidelberg and Marburg in the great days of Herrmann and Johannes Weiss. Furious debate raged from the Theological Society's Thursday evening-to-near-midnight sessions down to the Common Room fireplace (where lectures could be blissfully forgotten) and out to the private lodgings of students and into the Sub-warden's room in the New College Settlement, and it flared up again under the stars in the precincts of Braidburn Crescent, while in the springtime controversy was renewed in long walks and talks on the Pentlands, where the mad March hares were outdistanced by mental runners like Cecil Simpson, Ross Husband and the brothers Baillie. The god of war claimed all too soon some of the keenest minds, but most of the heretics of that day were spared to become resolute defenders of the faith before the onrush of a new crop of theological liberals in America, Canada, and the East Neuk o' Fife.

Those were the days of great preachers in Edinburgh and moving occasions. Imprinted indelibly on the memory of first-year men was the opening celebration of Holy Communion in the Free High Church: the hallowing stillness, the lovely grey head of the venerable Principal (Alexander Whyte), the rich commanding voice, the arresting exuberance of phrase, the oft-repeated 'Who is a God like unto Thee, who pardoneth iniquity?', the breaking of the bread, the lifting of the cup, the interpreting words, the hush of souls each making his own solemn consecration. In the city pulpits John Kelman and J. R. P. Sclater were drawing students by the combined wizardry of the man and winsome-ness of the message. As theology claimed us, we stole of an evening to the quietude of St. Andrew's, Drumsheugh Gardens, where W. M. Macgregor (whose congregation dined at seven) preached to a select audience. As one hand toyed with his eyeglasses and emotion rippled over a face like Dante's, he held us spellbound as in unhurried sentences of choice diction he set before us (in sermons afterwards published under these titles) *Jesus Christ, the Son of God, Some of God's Ministries, Repentance unto Life*. Such influences flowed in upon the sensitive spirit of Donald Baillie. These, however, were but supplementary to the family pieties and the regular worship of South Morningside, where Dr C. A. Salmond so long and faithfully broke the bread of life.

In May 1914 the happy circle at Braidburn Crescent was broken. Peter, the youngest of the three brothers, had gone to India as a medical missionary. He had written his farewell to Edinburgh:

> Now on my heart is fallen a heaviness,
>   O City that I love, thy spires ascend
> In the clean air. . . . Now as I wend
>   My journey here, how every stone can send
> Returning dreams of some old happiness!
>   And ye few friends who knew with me so well
> To tread the habitations of our dreams,
>   And some who hardly guessed what hidden gleams
> Ye stirred within me—'tis a long farewell.

Surely he had Highland second sight when he wrote the requiem:

> When I have lain beneath the reeds,
>   Below the grasses and the streams,
> O take no pomp of mourning weeds,
>   But make a pall out of my dreams.

Peter was accidentally drowned in India before his work had well begun.

College days had ended for Donald Baillie in March 1913. When the last examination is over and a four years' close fellowship comes to an end, there are inevitable forebodings and an eager peering into the future. Many wondered whether the shy diffident student would find his real meed of appreciation in a Church where settlement was by the agonizing method of competitive preaching. Licensing took place on a spring evening in Roseburn Church, when Dr S. G. Maclennan laid upon us the gravity and grandeur of our vocation. Then we scattered to our assistantships, Donald going to North Morningside, where the able and alert Dr D. W. Forrest was minister. We little suspected that a few months later the war clouds were to threaten and all too soon break upon our heads. Donald had not the physique for a soldier, and the effort to serve with the Y.M.C.A. in France was cut short by illness. Happily even in the disorder there is a place for every man, and in the border parish of St. Boswells, whose minister had immediately gone on active service, there was need for a *locum tenens* and there Donald was to have the first real taste of the life-work he had inherited from his father. Would any deep impression be expected from the ministry of one as yet unordained, one who was just feeling his way? Yet over thirty years afterwards an old lady, listening to an Edinburgh preacher of note, confessed to closing her eyes with delight because the voice brought to her the illusion that she was hearing the accents of Dr Donald Baillie, who remained to her still the best loved of all her ministers and the best man she had ever known. In long walks in that delightful border country, always observant of the wild flowers and on the outlook for new specimens, following trails laden with history and romance, the young preacher began to discover his health firmed and his mind refreshed, while among a congenial people he received confirmation of his calling. I remember

6

him at his happiest on a Monday morning heading for Dryburgh Abbey, overflowing with good talk, opening up the theological problems that were always buzzing in his mind, turning easily to light-hearted chaff and those stories that he could tell with so fine a touch and so rich a tang. There was of course the odd terrifying moment that his friends knew to expect in those long talks with one whose mind was so furnished and so acute. An immature comment on a theological issue brought first the meditative scrutiny of those sharp eyes and then the sobering challenge: 'But does that really *mean* anything?'

The Scottish probationer had in those days to find a kirk of his own the hard way, journeying much and oft to this remote parish or to that quiet country town, mentally chewing a couple of sermons, spending uneasy nights in strange quarters, nervously racing through his much-thumbed discourses under critical eyes and then with relief on a Monday morning hastening down the by-lanes to the station. It was an even greater ordeal for a man who never knew when, because of a tree in the garden or a cat in the house, asthma would suddenly lay him low, gasping for breath. Donald Baillie had his share of waiting till in 1918 he was called to the United Free Church at Inverbervie on the Kincardineshire coast. This small town with its pebbly beach, its huddle of quiet homes, its busy mill, was one of the Montrose Burghs which in the days of Radical ascendancy sent John Morley to Westminster. In his *Recollections* he records one visit: 'Superb sunshine, broad and flashing on the floor of waters; sea, sky and air all vivid; sauntering on the shore with Wordsworth and Arnold in my pocket. . . . Bervie, hereafter a name of bliss.' The young preacher certainly had such days there. But there too he had other days heavy with the tragedies that come when clouds shut out the sun, and at Gourdon there was often sorrow on the sea.

7

Morley went on to Montrose and, in the Congregational Manse, found to his delight A. E. Garvie, able and learned. 'It did me good', he writes, 'to think of the bright light of thought, knowledge, interest, burning away on this far shore.' He would have found another such on a later day along the coast at St. Cyrus where James Hastings was working on his monumental dictionaries and encyclopaedia. And soon another such light sent out its beams from the United Free Manse at Bervie, where for five years Donald Baillie preached, pondered the problems of theology, and occasionally gathered them into articles for the *Expositor* and other journals, while at the same time entering deeply into the lives of millworkers, fishermen and artisans. I can picture him also among his young folk gaily engaging in a game of thought-reading or in 'the pencil and the ring', and in another mood in the soft light of a Sabbath evening at Gourdon where the wrinkled weather-beaten faces of men who go down to the sea in ships fasten intently on the preacher as he carries them away to the Lake of Galilee and the Master who alone can still the waves of the soul. To the Manse there his mother had also come to make her home with her son, and thence radiated a beauty of character and loveliness of spirit that won all hearts.

The county town of Cupar is the real hub of the Kingdom of Fife, bustling industrial Kirkcaldy notwithstanding. To St. John's Church there D. M. Baillie was inducted in 1923 and sustained till 1930 a pastorate of deepening power. It was not with much golf on the sloping hill of Tarvit that he acquired the habit of hitching one shoulder higher than another; his recreation was rather in long walks into the undulating countryside, watching with interest the rising walls of the sugar-beet factory, child of local enterprise, and the erection of the Transatlantic transmitters at Kemback. He loved his ample garden and made a portion of it (a tennis court) a rendezvous with his young people. He was punctilious in his pastoral rounds, having a living interest in people and following eagerly the fortunes of families that sent their sons to India, Canada, and elsewhere beyond the seas. He was particularly happy in his fellow-presbyters, especially with Ronnie Macaulay of Bonnygate, whose untimely death was like the loss of a brother. He had become in 1921 an examiner in Divinity at St. Andrews, where he had congenial fellowship with Principal George Galloway and George Duncan, a friend of college days. Here too began to take shape those studies which were to form the theme of the Kerr Lectureship to which he was appointed in 1926: *Faith in God and its Christian Consummation*. It was a wise choice of subject, calling as it did for his philosophical acumen and his practical interest in religion. A vast array of authors from Plato to Bernard Shaw are laid under tribute as this seeker after truth wrestles with the elusive angel of Faith. But the nearest solution to his problem is acknowledged in the dedication TO MY MOTHER. One is tempted to linger at that breakfast table at Cupar where she presided with such Victorian grace, responding with her gentle musical laugh as her son, in the exuberance of a Monday m orning, teased her unmercifully about her fabulous years and accused her playfully of letting her thoughts wander after her 'prodigal' in the far country of New York State while her home-staying lad had to sing out loud for even a little bit of marmalade for his bread! Then would tinkle a little bell, and Annie, the housemaid, would come in, and family worship would proceed, in which, as a friend expressed it, 'he made the phrases which are so often conventional seem a natural speech'.

Meantime the name of this scholar and preacher still in his early forties had travelled to the West, where on the ridge above Greenock and Glasgow sits Kilmacolm; and, being now called to St. Columba's Church there, Donald Baillie was for four further years to continue his preaching and teaching ministry among a people noted for their warmth and generosity. But not for long was he to enjoy there the partnership of his mother. At a picnic on Loch Lomondside she slipped and fell, fracturing a shoulder-blade, and died a few days later in a Glasgow nursing home. 'It is', wrote Lord Morley, in his *Life of Cobden*, 'the bitterest element in the vast irony of human life that the time-worn eyes to which a son's success would have brought the purest gladness are so often closed for ever before success has come.' But she did see achievement on the horizon for both her surviving sons, though one would have loved to see her beatific face looking with pride upon the installation in 1943, the centenary year of the Disruption, of her eldest son, the son of a Free Church minister, as Moderator of the re-united Church of Scotland.

Several colleges overseas had made tempting approaches to the minister of Kilmacolm. Edinburgh appointed him Examiner in Divinity in 1933 and St. Andrews conferred her honorary doctorate in Divinity. Then with the re-organization of the Theological Colleges consequent on Union there were established in the more than four hundred years old College of St. Mary's, St. Andrews, two new chairs, and to one of these Donald Macpherson Baillie came to teach Systematic Theology in 1934. There could have been no happier conjunction of man and office. To his mastery of philosophy he had added long years of reflection on the cruces of theology, and in his several pastorates he had developed both his own humanity and his understanding of the contemporary situation for which he was to train his students. His health needed careful husbanding, but the invigorating air of St. Andrews was not uncongenial. He loved the sea and never tired of the spectacle of the white horses prancing in the dazzling sunshine along the West Sands and of the rugged pier flashing with the scarlet gowns of students as they streamed down after morning service. A saunter along the shady walk of the Lade Braes to the music of the burn was just the tonic that sent him back refreshed to his arduous reading and composing. Specially congenial was the religious tradition of the ancient University symbolized by the venerable fabric of St. Salvator's Church, presenting to the quadrangle of the United College the open door of worship every day of the week. The broken fragments of the once noble Cathedral, the ruins of monastery and abbey, the pre-Reformation foundation of the University, were like daily pointers to the glory of the undivided Church, and framed in his mind the vision of the reunion of Christendom. And when in later years he packed his bag to preach in an English Cathedral or to have conference with leaders of the Church of England, he could hear as he turned stationwards into the road that leads from Magus Muir the warning rumble of the ghostly carriage of Archbishop Sharp.

Against that historic background went on the serious exercise of writing and delivering lectures. Sixty-five note-books, more large than small, testify to the scholar's diligence in every department of his subject, all written in his own firm hand. Students regarded him as the ideal lecturer, so clear and orderly was his presentation, in fact so lucid and persuasive that they sometimes chided themselves too late that they had not taken down every word of that deceptive simplicity. 'I never knew anyone', said a graduate, 'who was so completely absorbed in his lecture, or who so completely absorbed us that we were hardly aware of any mannerisms.' He loved the intimacy of the Seminar. He will always be associated in the minds of his students with the historic Dining Hall of the College. There against the background of old pewter platters on the carved stone mantelpiece he sat in his chair before the old oaken table and presided over the study of the Westminster Confession, drawing out skilfully the hesitant, finding far more in the fuzzy answer than the fumbling beginner dreamed of, occasionally puncturing by a single deft shaft a plausible proposition, often pleading for a less prejudiced view of another Church's position, summing up in a way that lifted the debate to a higher level and leaving the religious truth standing clear. Not that the flame always burned brightly. There was dreary scrub to traverse, and weariness falls even on the youthful at the end of a long forenoon of lectures. But every now and then he would make the familiar idea flash with a new significance, as on one occasion Robin Barbour records. Commenting on the phrase anent the Communion of Saints, 'they without us shall not be made perfect' (Heb. 11.40) he added simply, 'That's a humiliating thought for us.'

Absorbed as he was in the process of exposition, he was observant as well. 'It was not possible', comments one student, 'to be absent from class and not be noticed. After a lecture one day he accosted me with the remark: "Do you know, Mr ——, that you come to only one lecture in three?" ' And then, the rebuke delivered, he went on to inquire why. 'Is there something wrong?' The student got rather a surprise that the great teacher should trouble about what seemed small things. 'But,' he said, 'as always, Professor Baillie asked the right question.' One day, too, Hamish stole into class very quietly. Then, waking up to the fact that he had not his text-book with him, he tiptoed back to fetch it, only to hear, 'It's a pity, Hamish, that when you *do* come to class you can't bring your book with you.'

Acutely conscious that a theology was valueless unless it would 'preach', he was always bringing reason and argument to that practical test. He never forgot the debt he owed to the historical school that unveiled for him the Jesus of history, and in the light of that he unfolded his doctrine of God, his review of the Christological controversies, and indeed all his theology. It was inevitable that his thought should reach its culmination in *God Was in Christ*. As the months moved on and each class came closer to their teacher, they became conscious that this man was the embodiment of his theology. As one put it, 'I don't think I ever knew anyone whose teaching and whose life were so nearly the same thing. As he spoke of the paradox of grace you could see that it was true.' A New Zealander set down his impression in this way: 'You often have the adjective "staunch" applied to a Presbyterian; it is less often that "devout" is applied. Yet that is the kind of Presbyterian that Dr Baillie was, and it was that which attracted me most of all to him. Perhaps it is that trait which made him so greatly esteemed by people ranging from Baptists to advanced Anglo-Catholics. That devotion was also, I think, the clue to his approach to theology. Whereas the usual way to lecture about the Atonement, for example, is to give most of the time available to a history of the doctrine and to a discussion of the various types of Atonement theory, Dr Baillie covered all that in a few lucid lectures and then spent most of the available time upon what the Atonement really means for us and how we are to conceive it and speak of it to men today. It was that approach to his work—and to people—that made him what some traditions would call an admirable "Spiritual Director".'

The timeliness and brilliance of *God Was in Christ* set Donald Baillie in the front rank of world theologians. Impression followed impression of the book. Students began to come from the ends of the earth to sit at his feet, and what they got there brought still more. He gave the Forwood Lectures at Liverpool in 1947; the Moore Lectures at San Francisco during an extensive tour in 1952. On the

Continent the interest in his Christology was so great that one of his last tasks was to prepare, in reply to points raised in discussion, an extra chapter for a German edition. That such should be required was a signal honour. But it was the same unassuming gentleman who walked the streets of the city by the sea. And while pondering great issues he never could neglect the small things.

A deeply Christian concern had long constrained the busy professor to undertake many laborious extras. He would not shelter behind the plea 'This one thing I do.' Despite his frail margin of strength he had faith to add to his burden. First and foremost he was a faithful elder in Martyrs Church. When ominous clouds overhung Europe and refugees streamed to our shores, he accepted the chairmanship of the local refugee committee, and documents written in his own hand testified to his fastidious care for every detail. When war conscripted the youth of the land he took up for a year the Scottish Secretaryship of the Student Christian Movement. When military camps poured out into the streets of the old grey city youths with nowhere to go, it was he who initiated the opening of a Church hall for their comfort and guardianship. He was one of the first to appreciate and sponsor the Iona Community, seeing in that a movement that was soundly based on personal devotion and went out among men with the message of the Incarnation. When Sir Walter Moberly roused men to the falling Christian standards of our universities, he started and was the moving spirit in a Moberly Group in St. Andrews. Even when health was precarious he would not refuse the extra journey to preach for an old student. Not only ministers but ministers' wives wrote for advice. 'His letters', writes one, 'were always so true and direct. He never watered things down or sugared them up; the truth just stood, and I can't tell you how indebted I was personally. I feel as if I have lost my Father Confessor and in that I must be one of many.'

Students like Donald Baillie who were passing through New College in the first decades of the century were aware that Hugh Ross Mackintosh was producing his *magnum opus* on the Person of Christ. The Student Movement was calling for the evangelization of the world in this generation. Then loomed up with a significance we did not realize the World Missionary Conference of 1910. Over against the disintegrating force soon to appear in two world wars that Conference stood for the unity of the world in Christ. The blood-letting of nations and the tears of churches cried out from the ground for the elevation of the one reconciling power—Jesus Christ. So Donald Baillie, having caught the torch from his teacher of Dogmatic, gave his mind increasingly to Christology and produced in 1947 his masterpiece long to remain a classic in theology: *God Was in Christ*. Issuing from that central theme of the Christ, the Church, Grace and the Sacraments next drew the consuming interest of his thought. Thus he was ideally qualified for the Ecumenical Movement, the child of the Missionary Conference of 1910. Zeal for the extension of Christianity had passed into graver concern for the interior problems of the Church —her message, her nature, her sacraments, in the hope that a deeper understanding of these would contribute to the realization of the ideal of One Flock, One Shepherd. Possessing a mind of penetrating subtlety, a catholicity of spirit, a sympathetic insight into various traditions and a personality at once engagingly winsome and unmistakably devout, he was in his right place as a constructive statesman at the Lund Conference on Faith and Order in 1952. Along with John Marsh he edited the volume on Intercommunion, and he became Convener of the Church of Scotland Committee on Inter-Church Relations. These were but the first fruits of a harvest we had hoped for, but cannot now see.

The volume and quality of this life's work can only be explained by the fact that underneath were the Everlasting Arms. Nothing but the peremptoriness of an early morning train could persuade this man of God to omit family worship at his own table. Unfailingly by 8.40 each week day down College Street came the familiar figure in the old mackin-tosh, gown over his arm, often looking pale, ill and fragile, on his way to morning prayers in the University Chapel: others might steal a morning off, he with more excuse would not. When he was a worshipper, there was the promptness of the real participant in every response. When he himself conducted the service, we could not but be drawn closer by the tones of his voice and the sincerity of his words. In addressing a newly-ordained minister his final stress was on the danger of letting carefulness about many things cut out the one thing needful—personal devotion. Members of his own College year knew how faithfully each Saturday even-ing he would keep the vow of remembrance of each other before God. The Committee on Youth of the United Free Church produced a *Day-Book of Prayer* for the private use of young men and women: in that he was the guiding and sustaining hand. He knew full well how even the saintliest need the ladder of prayer. In that booklet mark the section, 'God and My Moods'. Mingled with his serenity and even elevation of spirit there were periods of desolation and reac-tion. It was not out of nothing that he would preach on Elijah under the juniper bush.

> Let me no more my comfort draw
> From my frail hold of Thee;
> In this alone rejoice with awe,
> Thy mighty grasp of me.

It was in Kennedy Gardens that the new Professor estab-lished his home in 1934. At the turn of the road you can see the blue hills of Angus, but the Celt with second sight looked further to the West and saw the Crask, a hill in his native Gairloch, and so named his abode. Then too appeared opportunely Thomson, one of the quietly competent who are content to give their talents to creating the comforts of a home and ask little else than the joy of taking care of the master of the house and seeing him dispense her home-made delicacies with a liberal hand. It became almost a pilgrims' hospice, that book-lined study with the eastern window and couthy fireplace. Students came in relays, Americans on post-graduate study, German professors, ecumenical churchmen, travelling secretaries, refugees, chapel preachers, Gifford Lecturers, bejantines thrown from their bicycles carried in for first-aid, when the scarlet gown tangled with the wheels, semis and tertians who had fallen into deep theological waters and came for spiritual guiding from the man who never lost his gift of sympathizing with youth and who had ever the patience that suffereth long and is kind, and the art that turns incipient tears into laughter and self-pity into new hope.

It was a fortunate circumstance that in coming to St. Andrews he had the large-hearted welcome and support of an old friend, Professor (later Principal) George S. Duncan and that in the same year W. R. Forrester came to be Professor of Christian Ethics and Pastoral Theology. Mrs Forrester was a cousin and played sister to the bachelor professor. There at 54 South Street under a portal guarded by two wise owls there was always open a second home where of a Friday evening, theological and academic cares thrust aside, Donald Baillie became happy as a child among the children. He had always a fascination for children. His impish humour, his elfish face as he told a yarn or pro-pounded a nonsense riddle or rattled off the latest limerick, or improvised some daft ploy—it was all irresistible and stirred the company into gales of laughter. He believed there must be a place in heaven for family fooling.

Those who listened to the four broadcast services at Easter 1954 (here printed) must have noted with what strain on his frail physical resources the preacher carried them through. It was a triumph of will power. Much of that winter he had been having treatment painful to endure for what was supposed to be fibrositis. After vacation he seemed in better health for the Whitsunday term, but in the cold summer a visit to Argyll and then to Germany did not bring the usual resilience. He could not take the long walks he had loved. It was hard to persuade him to submit to proper medical examination, but after near-collapse, at last he gave in and went to Maryfield Hospital, Dundee, where a serious condition was diagnosed. Professor Hunter exercised all his skill, but there was no response to the treatment. In spite of weakness he kept up his lifelong habit of attending punctiliously to correspondence and his eager and affectionate interest in news of his friends persisted to the very end. His humour did not fail, as when pointing to the ink-stains on the sheets he remarked with a rueful face that he ought to be sent to bed without supper. He passed away in his sleep on the morning of the last Sunday of October to join the higher company on the eve of All Saints Day. When the news was flashed across the seas a former student wrote thus: 'There is a note of joy and gratitude to God in the midst of all this bewilderment and sadness. No one has ever communicated more passionately and vividly to me the Christian hope of eternal life, and no one has ever more plainly borne the marks on him of its present reality. No one has ever more utterly died to himself in the service of His Lord. No one that I have known has ever been so much part of the evidence for the truth of the Christian gospel.'

Throughout the whole University there was genuine

grief. 'We all loved Donald. No one among us was so much loved.' That was the feeling of the Faculty. Martyrs Church was crowded with mourners on the day of the funeral. The prayers of Rev. J. G. Thornton fittingly voiced our gratitude to the God who gave. The weather was grim. The cortege moved slowly down North Street between lines of scarlet-gowned students mingled with the black of the St. Mary's men and the varied colours of academic hoods worn by the professors. The mace-bearers stood sentinel. It was sad beyond words, did we not have in our hearts a love that could not die and a faith in God that has its consummation in the knowledge that God was in Christ reconciling the world unto Himself.

Donald Baillie knew from the beginning what a sermon should be. I can recall his first student 'outline'. We wondered what this brilliant philosophy student would produce. A magnificently articulated structure with four heads and many subsections like a class essay? No, we saw on the blackboard a model outline of attractive simplicity and directness. And so his sermons continued all along. He kept a sermon register that breaks off at number 652. It is characteristic that the first entry bears the text: 'Whosoever shall not receive the Kingdom of God as a little child' (Luke 18.17). Connected series are limited to four or five at a time, except when he comes to the Apostle Paul, where he loses all restraint and runs on to fifteen. Then he suddenly turns to Martha and Mary and 'Which of them will love Him most.' As this notable ministry reaches maturity more deeply underlined become the notes of Grace, Forgiveness, the Glory of the Cross, Eternal Life, The Communion of Saints.

I
SERMONS PREACHED
IN ST. ANDREWS UNIVERSITY CHAPEL

1. TO WHOM SHALL WE GO?

From that time many of his disciples went back, and walked no more with him. Then said Jesus unto the twelve, Will ye also go away? Then Simon Peter answered him, Lord, to whom shall we go? Thou hast the words of eternal life.　　　　JOHN 6.66-68

I AM speaking today to many who stand at the very beginning of their university career. A few months ago you were still at school, schoolboys or schoolgirls. Now that is left behind for ever, and a new chapter begins, a chapter in which you will have greater independence than you have ever had before. In many ways you will have to make up your own minds, because you have reached the responsibilities of manhood and womanhood. For you this is a time of change, of development, of responsibility, of decision, of choice. And it may be that in the deepest matters some of you are conscious of that in a way you have never been before.

You have been brought up, many of you, perhaps most of you, in the Christian tradition, and it may be that hitherto you have accepted it somewhat passively, without making it very deeply your own or making up your minds about it. But now you have reached a stage when that is hardly possible any longer, because childhood is past and you have to choose your own path. At that stage some young people simply drop the Christianity in which they were brought up, perhaps even quite consciously turn back from Christ and give up their Christian heritage. Others accept it and make it their own more than they ever did before, realizing in a new way what it means, and finding in Christ the Way, the Truth and the Life, for themselves.

It is to symbolize that situation that I take these familiar words from St. John's Gospel. 'From that time many of his disciples went back, and walked no more with him. Then said Jesus unto the twelve, Will ye also go away? Then Simon Peter answered him, Lord, to whom shall we go? Thou hast the words of eternal life.'

What else can we turn to but the Gospel of Christ? That is what Simon Peter's question amounts to. And I want to take it and break it up into three questions, which, taken one after the other, make an argument (so far as this can be done by argument) for accepting your Christian heritage by a personal faith of your own.

(1) *What would life be without some high purpose?* I do not say at once without the Christian religion: I'll come to that later. But to begin with, what would life be without some high serious purpose, some gleam to follow, some dream, some endeavour, to lift it above the mere struggle for existence and give it a meaning?

What would even university life be without that? I wonder if you have ever asked yourself why you are at a university, or what a university is for. It isn't a perfectly simple question with an obvious answer. It is a question about which a great deal of thinking has been done in recent years in many quarters, just because people have realized that without some high guiding purpose university life cannot continue to be sound. In various ways and in various parts of the world, in our time, universities have been in danger of losing their souls for want of a high purpose, a sound principle, a wholesome philosophy of life. But apart from these high and difficult problems, why are you at a university yourself? What is the justification of it? What do you want to make of it? Do you think of it as simply a necessary vocational training, because you have to earn your living afterwards? Or do you think of it merely as an opportunity for having a good time? Can you forget that

24

in many parts of the world just now there are fellow-students of yours to whom all these things look very different because of what they have to suffer? In recent years there have been vast numbers of young men and women in the world who have been driven desperately to ask the question whether life has any meaning at all. Perhaps they gave their hearts to some big movement which captivated their youthful ideal-ism, and then it failed them, they saw through it and were disillusioned; and they are looking for something, wondering what there is to live for. Moreover there are great numbers of students in Europe and Asia today who have to live their lives and pursue their studies in conditions which would seem to us quite impossible, with shortage of money and food and rooms and books and time and everything that university life would seem to require.

That is the world we are living in. Surely in this present age more than in most ages young people like you are bound to awaken and ask themselves what they are living for. In such a world you can't accept all your privileges compla-cently and set out to have a good time for yourselves. You can't take life like that. If you do, it goes bad, it goes rotten on your hands, for want of a high purpose in such a tragic world.

There is a golden sentence at the very end of one of Nansen's books about his polar explorations, this closing sentence: 'What would life be without its dreams?' He was thinking of his dreams of Arctic icefields, to explore which he had suffered such unimaginable hardships of polar ad-venture, and thought it well worth while, far better than an easy life at home. Later in life he dreamed an even nobler kind of dream, and carried it out in his great work of rescuing refugees and minorities in Central Europe after the First World War. He need not have done it. He might have lived on his dreams of past achievements and the deathless fame he had won. Why then did he court fresh troubles for the dream of a better Europe? Again the answer is: what would life be without its dreams? And I can ask you the question with even greater force in this your day and generation, this age that is so confused and so tragic. In such a world, what would life be for anyone of you without some high purpose, some ideal? That is my first question.

(2) *What would an ideal be without religion?* That is to say: *without God.* What would life's dreams be if they were only human dreams, with no God behind them?

You will perhaps wish impatiently to remind me that many an honest sceptic has had high moral ideals, and that, God or no God, our moral convictions stand fast. You will tell me that many who do not profess to believe in God have a greater social concern, a finer devotion to the cause of reform among their fellow-men, than many Christians. You will perhaps remind me that the great Dr Nansen himself was an unbeliever, and yet he worked out his dreams for the relief of suffering humanity in a way that would put most of us to the blush. Yes, indeed. But I wonder how long that kind of thing can last—high ideals and noble service without any faith. For one generation, perhaps, and then mainly by living unconsciously on the religious capital of the last generation. I am sure that has often been true in circles of high-minded intellectuals who lost their faith. And many of them have themselves been conscious that it was a sad business, trying to maintain a high purpose without any religious belief. Didn't one of the great agnostics of last century say that he would give his right hand to be able to believe what Christians believe? And as for the books that try to work out such a way of life, a moral ideal without any religious faith, there have been many such books, serious and honest and high-minded. But the more sincere they are,

26

the more tragic they are, because it is in the end a tragic business to try to have morality without religion, to cherish an ideal without God.

But better than any books, life itself will drive you to see it. Perhaps it has driven you already, and what you would really like to ask me impatiently is why I keep talking of ideals. You are tired of that word. I don't wonder. It is a word that lets us down. You get hold of an ideal of character for yourself, and you strive to mould your character upon it. That is something to live for. And then presently you discover that, with all your concentration on cultivating an ideal character, you have only succeeded in making yourself more self-centred than ever, which is just what might have been expected, because you have been thinking so much of yourself. That way seems hopeless. Then perhaps, in disgust of yourself, you turn outwards to the dream of an ideal of humanity, to the service of mankind and the crusade of making the world a better place with a nobler happier breed of man. That sounds better and more wholesome. But very soon you begin to discover that the world is a much bigger problem than you imagined, and far more difficult to transform and redeem. How many high-minded humanists and idealists have made that discovery in our own generation! There is something so far wrong with the world that all our noblest planning can't put it right. You begin to tell yourself that all your little endeavours seem to make no difference, they count for nothing. Perhaps you even begin to tell yourself that you have no right to talk of transforming the world: you have more need to be transformed yourself. And there you are again, back at the thought of yourself. And yet you are sick of yourself.

What then? You can't go back to a life without ideals: that would be worst of all. But what then? What do you want now? To what can you go forward?

Is it possible that you want God? Can you go forward to what we call religion?

Suppose it should be true that the ultimate reality of this universe is not humanity, but God. Suppose it should be true that all that you call your ideals comes from Him, from His will, from His love, calling you and claiming you; and that all your unrest, all your questing, is the work of His Holy Spirit in your heart. Suppose that underneath all the chaos of human history there is an unseen and eternal Kingdom of God, which He is continually carrying forward, and that God Himself has redeemed and is redeeming the world. Suppose that when you have lost and betrayed all that you call your ideals, God has not given you up, but will forgive you and accept you and even use you and send you out again—not to realize an ideal or to redeem the world (for you can't do these things), but to do His will and serve His Kingdom.

Wouldn't that make everything worth while again? A new beginning every day in the mercy of God, and endless endeavours to do God's will in the service of mankind, a life in which these little endeavours can't be wasted and won't be lost, because they are part of the invincible campaign of God's everlasting Kingdom. That changes everything, your personal life and all your service of mankind. It is all transformed, because of God. That is what you want. And that is religion. So I ask (and now you can understand it): What would an ideal be without religion? That is my second question.

(3) *What would religion be without Christ?* That is the climax. I have not until now spoken of Christ in my argument, but of course it has all been pointing to Him.

There have indeed been many religions in the world besides the Christian religion; and I believe something of God's truth has been in every one of them, for some race of mankind, in its own time and place, as men were able to receive it. But after all, when it comes to the vital issue for you and me, standing where we are, what other religion is there to be seriously considered except the Gospel of Christ? When it isn't an easy-chair argument or a debating society, but a desperate need of something to live by in this chaotic world, what else is there but the religion of Christ?

All those things I have just been hypothetically describing as the things that we desperately need—the love of God to sinful men, the redemption of the world, the forgiveness of sins, the opportunity of new beginnings, the Kingdom of God, which calls us to its service among our fellows, and which is invincible and everlasting—all that pattern of belief and life is not simply *any* religion or *every* religion: it is the religion of Christ, the Gospel of Christ.

And to crown it all: if the Gospel is true, then not only is the ideal an eternal reality in heaven, not only is the dream an invincible purpose of God, but also: the Word became flesh and dwelt among us on earth: God Himself was incarnate in Jesus Christ and bore the sin of the world for our salvation.

If the Gospel is true, I said. I haven't proved it to be true. I haven't even tried to do that. I don't think anybody can exactly prove it, in black and white on paper. This conviction comes in a different way, when in practice you face up to it. But isn't it something to face up to? It isn't irrelevant. It matters immensely. It is worth believing in. What would life be without a high purpose? What would a high purpose be without religion? and what would religion be without Christ? To whom can we go but unto Him?

That is the Christian inheritance about which you have to make up your mind.

Eternal God, who hast set before us life and death for

our choice, and hast given us Jesus Christ to be the way, the truth and the life, help us to enter that way, to receive that truth, and to live by that life. Suffer us not to miss the purpose of our creation, but make us to be sons and daughters of thine and servants of Thy Kingdom. Through the same Jesus Christ our Lord.

2. YOUR SONS AND YOUR DAUGHTERS
SHALL BE PROPHETS

And it shall come to pass afterward, that I will pour out my spirit upon all flesh; and your sons and your daughters shall prophesy, your old men shall dream dreams, your young men shall see visions.

JOEL 2.28

This is that which was spoken by the prophet Joel; And it shall come to pass in the last days, saith God, I will pour out of my Spirit upon all flesh; and your sons and your daughters shall prophesy, and your young men shall see visions, and your old men shall dream dreams.

ACTS 2.16, 17

'YOUR sons and your daughters shall prophesy, shall be prophets.' What does that mean? What were those prophets whom we meet so frequently in the Bible? What was a prophet? Not simply a man who had a mysterious power of predicting future events, not a kind of fortune-teller or crystal-gazer; but something much better. In the highest sense of the word, a prophet was a man who could tell the people about God's purposes, at first hand, because he knew God for himself and could hear God's voice. In ancient Israel the common run of people did not expect to be able for themselves to enter into those mysteries. They took their religion with the crowd, at second hand. What else could they do? They were content to believe what they were taught, and do as they were told—carry out their religious duties as decent members of the community. That was enough for most people. But sometimes—once or twice in a generation—there would appear a man who was different from the rest, a man who was obviously meant to be a spokesman of God. Somehow the Spirit of God was upon him, he could know God for himself, and enter into some

31

of God's secrets, and tell other people about God's mind and will. But of course that could only be one man in a thousand, nay perhaps one in a hundred thousand, one in a generation, a man apart, a friend of God, a prophet.

And now, against that background, I wish to set before you three very remarkable scenes from different parts of the Bible.

(1) The first is away back in the early days when the Israelites were wandering through the wilderness under the *leadership of Moses*. One day (so the story goes) Moses their leader stood and said that he wished everybody could have God's Spirit and be a prophet. He said it impulsively, in a generous moment, to show that he wasn't selfish or jealous in these matters. He was a great prophet himself, and one day when two other men began to set up as independent prophets, outside his authority, his friends told him, and expected him to put a stop to it. But he was too noble for that; and he cried out, with a fine touch of imagination: 'Are you jealous for my sake? I wish to God that all God's people were prophets, and that he would put his spirit on every one of them.' Splendid generosity! But of course it was not intended as a practical proposition—that the common run of people, the rank and file of humanity, should blossom out like that, and be able to talk about God for themselves. Yet was it not a remarkable utterance?

(2) My second scene is still more remarkable. A thousand years later another great man stood up and said that the thing would one day come true. He may not have been actually thinking of Moses' words, but that was the substance of it. It was *the man called Joel*. And he was convinced of it.

Now it is usually a dangerous thing to make sweeping statements about the future and the changes which the future will bring in human affairs. Such predictions often turn out quite wrong, for, as Chesterton says, history is very fond of

playing the game of 'cheat-the-prophet'. But this man Joel
was absolutely sure the thing was going to happen—that the
time would come when all sorts of ordinary people would
know God for themselves and have His Spirit. He was
convinced that God had told him, and he put the words in
God's mouth. 'It shall come to pass afterward, that I will
pour out my spirit upon all flesh (*i.e.*, on all kinds of people);
and your sons and your daughters shall be prophets, your
old men shall dream dreams, your young men shall see
visions; and even upon the servants and upon the handmaids
in those days will I pour out my spirit.' What an extraordinary thing to say! How risky it must have sounded! To
talk of ordinary people, young fellows and young girls,
labouring folk and all sorts, having God's Spirit just as truly
as the prophets, having heavenly visions and being able to
talk about God for themselves! Joel did not say when he
expected it to happen, or how long it would be, but he did
say that it would come. And how remarkable! How
unlikely!

(3) But here is the third scene, still more remarkable and
unlikely. Four hundred years later another great man stood
up and said that the thing had now actually just come true.
It was *Simon Peter, on the Day of Pentecost*, as recorded in our
text. And he said it because of things his own eyes were
seeing, and everybody around him was also seeing, that
summer day. It was in that same historic city of Jerusalem,
where Joel had been a prophet. But now most people would
have told you that Jerusalem's great days were past, and it
was a day of small things, spiritually. Most people would
have told you that nowadays there were no great prophets,
and that religion was at a pretty low ebb. But that summer
day wonderful things were seen in Jerusalem: a host of
people met together in religious fellowship, all sorts and
conditions of men and women, but most of them very

ordinary-looking, like the weather-beaten fisherman Simon Peter himself. And there they all were, eager and joyful, united in a new and wonderful fellowship, with a new light on their faces, because a new and supernatural thing had come into their lives. Moreover it was not a mere passing excitement. Some of the onlookers said it was, and shrugged their shoulders. But Peter knew better, and he spoke out. This was the work of God. What had happened to these people was that GOD had come into their lives as a great reality, and given life a new meaning and purpose. Hitherto they had taken their religion in a second-hand conventional way, as a venerable custom. But now it is different. Now they have a faith of their own, and it has brought them a new fellowship and a new courage, and they are prepared to go anywhere, in spite of danger, and testify to what they believe. God has come into their lives. And so Peter stood up and said: 'It has come true at last. This is what was predicted by the prophet Joel: It shall come to pass, saith God, that I will pour out of my Spirit upon all flesh; and your sons and your daughters shall be prophets, and your young men shall see visions, and your old men shall dream dreams. And even on my servants and on my handmaidens I will pour out in those days of my Spirit.' The wonderful thing had actually happened. The knowledge of God had become a thing for everybody.

What had happened to bring it about? Is it possible to give any answer to that question? Was there anything special, to which we can point? Yes, of course there was. There was—Jesus Christ. Jesus of Nazareth had lived among men in Palestine; and wherever He went, with His words and works, His faith and love, His sense of the presence of God—wherever He went, God became real, and ordinary people could understand Him. Ordinary people, who had never expected to be able to understand the mysterious things the prophets talked of—now they could, as they listened to Jesus. That did not go on for ever, for presently Jesus got into trouble with the authorities, and was condemned and crucified. But very soon afterwards His people discovered that that did not make an end of it. He was not dead, He was alive, and now He was present in a more wonderful way even than when He was with them in the flesh. This was something new in mankind's knowledge of God, and it was something that anybody could have anywhere through the story of Jesus. It was just the Spirit of God, which had been supposed to be confined to the prophets and a few exceptional men, now coming into the hearts of all sorts of people, if only they would understand it and receive Him. That was the difference Christ had made, and that people realized on the Day of Pentecost, and that made Peter say that the old forecast of Joel had at last come true.

Now that is a very old story. Can we translate it into the language and the interests of our own modern world? Let us try, with the aid of a little imagination.

(1) You take your seat in a railway compartment. In the opposite corner sits a labouring man, reading his newspaper. You look at him and try to picture the life he leads. A rough bare life, you think; hard work all day, a quiet pipe in the evening, a football match to watch on a Saturday afternoon; and if he is a particularly decent man, he goes to church once in a while on a Sunday morning. So you sum up his life. Is that all? I wonder. When the man puts down his paper and leans back and shuts his eyes, what is he thinking of? Perhaps he is thinking of GOD. Perhaps he is bringing the light of his faith in God to bear upon the great issues he has been reading about in his newspaper—labour troubles, party politics, war and peace among the nations. Perhaps he is connecting all these things with the God he believes in. Why not? He is a working man. So was Jesus. And you

don't know what depths of Christian faith there may be in the heart and life of that ordinary man.

(2) Or you go into a shop in the city. A girl at the counter serves you. What does she care for, except to get on as well as she can in her own line, and meanwhile get as much fun as she can out of her wages when working hours are over, a round of rather selfish and empty pleasures filling up her evenings and week-ends? And that is all. Is it? It may be. But it may be also that that girl has visions and dreams that would go straight to the heart of Jesus Christ Himself. It may be that behind the scenes of what seems a very commonplace existence there is a brave unselfish life of burden-bearing for other people, sustained perhaps by the fellowship of the Church of Christ and by a living faith in God.

You can imagine any number of cases. I think perhaps it would be best of all if we could have a glimpse of a Christian congregation at worship in one of the younger churches in Africa or India or China: a mixed company of men and women and children of different races, different colours, different castes and classes, different languages and degrees of education, and indeed every conceivable difference on the natural plane; and yet meeting together on a deeper level, with one heart and one soul, worshipping God in a supernatural unity, as one family of His; because they all have one thing in common—they have God, they have Christ, they have the communion of the Holy Spirit.

All these things are happening in the world, in those ways that I have been picturing and in countless other ways that you can picture for yourselves. And it is just what Joel said would happen, and what Peter said had begun to happen, coming true again in new ways in the twentieth century. 'I will pour out of my Spirit upon all flesh; and your sons and your daughters shall be as prophets, and your young men shall see visions, and your old men shall dream dreams; and even on my servants and on my handmaids I will pour out in those days of my Spirit.'

In closing, let me ask two questions.

(1) Is all that as true of our generation as it has been of some past generations in Scotland? Is it happening as much as it used to happen—old men dreaming noble dreams of God's Kingdom, young men and women seeing heavenly visions of what God has done in Christ, and being captivated as His disciples? Is it happening as much today? I hope it is. I am sure it *is* happening. It is happening in quite new ways in Africa and India and China. But it is happening also in Scotland; in different ways, perhaps, from the ways of our forefathers, and expressed in different language (for one generation is not like another); but I am sure it is happening just as truly, because God is for everybody, Christ is for everybody, in every age.

(2) My second question is: What about ourselves? What about our own congregation? Have we in our midst the fellowship of the Holy Spirit, uniting us on the deepest level, because God has spoken to each one of us in Christ? What would the life of the Church of Christ, what would the life of this country of Scotland, have been through all the centuries without that kind of thing happening quietly and deeply among all sorts of people, from cottage to castle up and down the land? Friends, let us not miss it in our day and generation. The one aim and end of all we have inherited, all we have been taught, in our Christian homes and in the Church of Christ, is that we should, each one, and all in fellowship, come to have Jesus Christ as our own Lord and Master, the eternal God as our Father and our Friend, in the communion of the Holy Spirit.

3. REALITY IN RELIGION

And Elijah came unto all the people, and said, How long halt ye between two opinions? if the Lord be God, follow him; but if Baal be God, then follow him. And the people answered him not a word.
1 KINGS 18.21

If ye then be risen with Christ, seek those things which are above, where Christ sitteth on the right hand of God. COLOSSIANS 3.1

IT is often said nowadays that we live in a realistic age, in which people will have reality or nothing. That is often said especially about the rising generation. They are far more realistic than were their fathers or grandfathers. They are much more impatient of convention and make-believe. Well, I dare say the same thing has been said before of other young generations; and it is a somewhat delusive thing to make such sweeping comparisons and contrasts between one's own generation and past ones. There may be far less difference than we imagine. But in the present case there does seem to be something in the contrast. There does seem to have been a change, since what we used to call pre-war days (before 1914). Many respectable conventions have broken down. 'Convention' is not a very reputable word nowadays, and the younger generation would much rather be thought unconventional and realistic. They will ask questions about things that were supposed to be settled, and they will not be put off with old rules, venerable taboos. They want answers, they want reasons. They are impatient of what, in the army slang of the last war, used to be called eye-wash. They ask for reality. At least that is the impression they often make, and they wouldn't be sorry to make that impression. And that explains a good many things; and it sometimes frightens older people.

I want to begin by making two remarks about it—both of them perhaps a little unexpected.

In the first place, the change is not a bad thing. It is a good thing. If the new generation is really less bound by convention, more eager for reality, that may be disturbing, it may bring dangers and raise problems. But in itself surely it is a sign of life and health and courage and honesty. However useful conventions may be in their place, life should not be guided by convention, and people should not be afraid to ask honest questions, and it is a good thing to be somewhat independent of what people think, and to break away from stuffy respectability into the open air of truth and reality. I'm not going to flatter the rising generation, as you will soon see. But if what I have been saying does in some measure describe a present-day tendency—if there is that break-away from convention towards reality—surely we needn't be sorry. It may create complications, and upset some things. But we shouldn't be afraid of it. It is a good thing to be realistic. That is my first remark.

And my second is this: I believe a great many people in the present rising generation are far less realistic than they imagine—especially in their religion. I believe many of the people who would rejoice most to call themselves unconventional are far more bound and led by convention than they know. They may have shaken off one set of conventions, but they are quite enslaved by the conventions of their own circle, in the timidest kind of way. They do not carry their realism anything like far enough. If they did, they would be far better Christians than they are. They like to think they are living in the open air of truth and reality; but they are terribly unrealistic and conventional when it comes to the deeper things—the things of God. They take these things in such a timid respectable way. Balzac says, in description of one of his characters: 'He believed in God as gentlemen believe.' Isn't that common? But it isn't any use. It isn't the real thing. The real thing is far too big, far too searching, far too exhilarating, to be taken like that. It is neck or nothing. You can't play at it. And so I say: What a pity that so many people who like to be realistic aren't more realistic in their religion!

This text from the Old Testament shows us a genuine realist standing up to people of his time with that challenge. There was plenty of religion in the country. The people were quite keen on it. But they had no idea that it must be neck or nothing. They 'believed in God as gentlemen believe'. In fact, they were exceedingly gentlemanly about it. Of course they had every intention of worshipping the Lord God of their fathers, for old times' sake. But then it had also become a fashion of the time to worship the Baal who was the god of their Tyrian neighbours. They didn't notice that the two could not mix—morally. The king had married a Tyrian princess, and it seemed a graceful gesture to begin to worship her god too. 'Why not? You must move with the times! You mustn't be narrow minded, especially in religion. A man can worship God as he chooses, and religion is a very good thing anyway, and the more you can have of it the better. So why not worship both Baal and Jehovah?' I'm sure that is how they spoke. It will occur to you that it is very like what so many people have been doing in Germany in recent years—trying to combine Christianity with the new Teutonic Paganism. Perhaps it is. A chapter like this, about Elijah on Mount Carmel, must have been frequently read and expounded, with a burning message, in faithful German pulpits of recent years. But are you sure it isn't even more like what so many people are doing in England or Scotland—playing at religion, dabbling in the things of God? That is what the people of Israel were doing. They would gaily worship either Baal or Jehovah, turn about or both together, because neither the one nor the other meant much to them. It was all so deeply conventional, though they didn't see it.

The one realist of that situation was Elijah—we can see it now (whatever we make of the rest of the strange story). Round about him were all those complacent people, following the fashions in their dress and in their worship. And there was he, a rugged figure, a man of the desert, roughly clad; a prophet, with flaming eyes and honest speech, without fear or favour for either people or king. (We may be sure he did not enjoy being against people: he was a lonely tragic figure, sometimes acutely depressed. But he had to be real.) That day on Mount Carmel he stood up and said: 'How long halt ye between two opinions? if the Lord be God, follow him; but if Baal be God, then follow him.' As much as to say: 'How long are you going to play at religion? It is too big a thing to play at. Remember that you are dealing with GOD, and do not call upon Him at all unless you mean it. You can't have it both ways with God. It must be one or the other, and you will find that out as soon as you start being real.' So spoke Elijah the realist. And see what comes next: 'And the people answered him not a word.' They couldn't. They didn't know where they were. He had pricked the bubble of their conventional religion, and there was nothing left.

Let us imagine what a prophetic spirit like Elijah might say to us today, by way of challenge to our Christian profession. It might be something like this. 'Why do you turn out on a Sunday morning for what we call the public worship of God? Is it because your heart is hungry for God? Does it make any real difference to you? Does it help you through the week? And if not, why not? Do you really believe in God? If there is a god at all, He can't be such a nonentity that He makes no difference, one way or the other, to those who believe in Him. But do you really believe in Him? On Monday as well as on Sunday? And if so, do your thoughts often turn to Him? Do you pray much to Him? Do you confess your sins? Or are you in that respect running away from reality? Do you take much trouble to read the Bible, which contains His Word, and to understand it as you would wish to understand any subject that vitally affected your career? What do you make of the story that is told in the four Gospels? Have you ever reckoned with that central figure of Jesus Christ that appears in the story? Do you believe what people say about Him—the things that are implied in every bit of our worship? And if so, what are you going to do with Him? Or even with His teaching? Was He right about the secret of life? So right that you mean to trust your life to His proposals? This great supernatural business that He stood for, this reckless enterprise for which it was worth while to be crucified, this Kingdom of God—do you believe in it? Do you believe what is pictorially symbolized in the story of the Ascension, that the things for which He stood are enthroned at the heart of the universe, as the only things that matter? And if so, do you rise and follow Him? Or have you just a conventional religion? 'If you are risen with Christ, seek those things which are above, where Christ sitteth on the right hand of God.' If Jesus is Lord, then follow Him.

That is how the prophet would put the challenge to us. And could you meet it? Would the result be what it was that day on Mount Carmel: 'The people answered him not a word'?

There is one answer that some people would be disposed to give. They would say: 'You are expecting too much of young people. It isn't natural in the days of youth to be deeply concerned about religion and the great things of the Kingdom of God. That will come later. It belongs to maturer age. It doesn't happen to young people.' Doesn't it? Yes, indeed, it does. It is quite especially to young people that it does happen. That is so true that some psychologists have actually spoken of conversion as 'a phenomenon of adolescence'. No doubt that is misleading. The very word 'conversion' can be misleading, because it has so often been misused by people who imagined that religion must come to everybody in the same sudden kind of experience— forgetting that the wind bloweth where it listeth, and God's spirit works in many ways. The very word 'religion' can be most misleading, when people think of religion as a kind of pious extra, a curious bit of emotional experience which has to be added on to life, for the people who are built that way —the people who have 'the religious temperament'. What nonsense! That is not how the Bible talks of religion. In fact, the Bible hardly uses that word—perhaps we use it too much. The Bible does not talk about religion, but about God: God's will, God's law, God's love, God's forgiveness, God's call, God's ways with men. And what is religion but becoming aware of all that and letting it govern our lives? Sometimes we run away from it all, and that means running away from reality. But sometimes it overtakes us, and God comes into our lives, and that is religious reality.

Now that can, by God's grace, happen to anyone at any age. But it is in the days of youth that it most commonly begins to happen to a man, if it is ever going to happen to him at all. If you read the life stories of those who have been seekers and finders, saints and servants of God, you will discover that in most cases it was in the days of young manhood or womanhood that they were first gripped by the great realities of the Kingdom of God—awakened out of the conventional acceptance of an inherited religion, and made to open their own lives to God. To young people nowadays I believe that often comes through an acute realization of the woes and sorrows of the world. Surely it must be happening in that way to many people just now, and to many young people, unless in these testing times they are running away from reality. But however it happens, what is the good of what we call religion, to young or old, until that begins to happen to it? You must have reality. 'If the Lord be God, then follow Him.'

I have spoken of Elijah the realist. But after all, the great realist in religion is Jesus Christ, as we find Him in the Gospel story. It was just because He could not tolerate shams in religion, because He would go piercing through conventions and make straight for reality, that the respectably religious people could not tolerate Him and got Him crucified. He loved men with all His heart, and longed with all His heart to draw them to Him, for their salvation and the service of God's Kingdom. But He did not want merely conventional followers, or He might have had far more disciples than He had. They sometimes offered. But He knew that it was no use—no use to Him and no use to them. So He often said some very searching thing, and it sometimes scared them away—as it sometimes scares us when we read the Gospels. He took the risk of that, rather than the risk of unreality.

He did not scare away blunderers and seekers, perplexed people and doubters, publicans and sinners, or anyone who really wanted to follow. There were Peter and Andrew, James and John and Matthew. Sometimes they were afraid of Him. Often they couldn't understand Him. But they knew in the bottom of their hearts that He was the very incarnation of truth and reality, and that it must be neck or nothing. So they left all and followed Him. And their whole testimony shouts to us: 'How long halt ye between two opinions? if Jesus is Lord, then follow Him'.

4. BOUGHT WITH A PRICE

Ye are not your own. For ye are bought with a price. Therefore glorify God.   1 CORINTHIANS 6.19, 20

ST. PAUL was dealing with one particular moral question—he was talking about the sins of the flesh. There was much need to talk about that in writing to a city like Corinth, even if the people to whom he was writing were Christians. They had not been Christians very long, and they were still sometimes disposed to imagine, along with their neighbours, that the sins of the body were hardly sins at all. 'A man can do what he likes with his own body.' Well, that is just what St. Paul denies. He says it is a lie. He says: That can't possibly be true for Christians. For your body is not your + own. It belongs to God, just as much as your soul. It has been redeemed by Christ, just as much as your soul. A price has been paid for it. It doesn't belong to yourself. It's God's temple, and it has to be kept holy for Him. 'Don't you know', he says, 'that your body is a temple of the Holy Spirit which is in you and which you have from God? You are not your own. You were purchased with a price. Therefore glorify God in your body.'

If I wished to speak to you of that subject today, what better words could I find than Paul's? What better secret is there for dealing with the lusts of the flesh than to learn to reverence the body—our own bodies and the body of every fellow-creature—because the body is created to be servant of the spirit, and both body and spirit to be servants of God?

But I wish, on this Founder's Day, to make a much wider application of St. Paul's words, as indicating the whole spirit in which we are going to live our lives in the world. I think

45

St. Paul's argument here is the best answer that could possibly be given to the spirit of selfish individualism that creeps into so many lives, young and old. That is what I wish to speak of—that selfish individualism and how mean it is, and what we need to put in its place. And I can't do better than take in succession the three simple clauses of this Pauline text. 'Ye are not your own. For ye are bought with a price. Therefore glorify God.'

(1) *'Ye are not your own.'* A strange thing to say. You don't belong to yourselves. You are not your own property. If it is true, then the whole philosophy of individualism comes tumbling down like a house of cards.

Of course the word *'individualism'* has so many different senses, and we must not be confused. But think for a moment of this selfish individualism of which I am speaking, and you will recognize it, though it isn't very respectable. Its motto is: 'My life is my own, and I can do what I like with it. It's a good thing to have, and I'm not going to let the claims of other people spoil it for me. I have a right to my own way, my own self-realization, and I'm going to have it.' Doesn't that spirit, conscious or unconscious, creep into many lives, especially young lives?

Now I know what a wonderful thing it is to awaken, in the days of youth, to the realization that one has a life of one's own to live. Age after age that happens, when a lad or a lass is emerging out of boyhood or girlhood into manhood or womanhood. There comes that wonderful new keen sense of individuality. The young fellow bringing home his own earnings for the first time, or going away to live in rooms for the first time—growing up, having to make all sorts of little decisions for himself instead of depending on his parents, going out into the world to live as a man among one's fellows—what a new vista it opens up! An individuality of one's own, friends of one's own, choices of one's own, a life to live. The young fellow realizes that, however little else he may have, he has this, and it is wonderful.

Well, I say, it ought to be wonderful. All that is right and good, the very stuff out of which character is made, when it is captured for the enterprise of the Christian life. But instead of that, it sometimes blossoms out into a calculating selfishness. The keen sense of individuality becomes perverted into a mean heartless individualism, in which a young soul forgets everybody except itself. A lad gets such a keen sense of his own importance that other claims fade out: he must cut a figure himself, have his own success, his own pleasure. Or a girl begins to carve out her own life, shakes off encumbering responsibilities, develops a sort of heartlessness to those who might have some claim upon her. Lad or lass, it isn't an unfamiliar picture, is it? But it isn't a beautiful picture. That kind of individualism is just selfishness: hard mean irresponsible selfishness. And is there anything uglier than that, in a young life? Is there anything uglier than the particular brand of ingratitude and selfishness that you sometimes see in young people? Unless perhaps it be the pedestrian middle-aged selfishness to which it usually leads as the years pass. That is what it leads to, and that is perhaps even uglier still: men and women living among their fellows with no thought but their own security and prosperity, without sympathy or compassion or imagination or any sense of social responsibility. Surely that is the unloveliest kind of middle life for anybody. And then, middle life too passes; 'and age comes on, uncheered by faith or hope'—the saddest thing in the world.

That is individualism. It is a philosophy of life, conscious or unconscious. 'My life is my own, and all I have is my own, and I can do what I like with my own.'

Well, now, I say, with St. Paul, it isn't true. It is based on a lie. Your life, with all its riches, does not belong to yourself.

That is the meaning we must put into this first clause of our text. 'Ye are not your own.' But what reasons can we give? That brings us to the second clause.

(2) '*For ye are bought with a price.*' Your life is not your own private property, because a price has been paid for all that makes it what it is, and it isn't you that has paid the price.

What does that mean? A whole world of meaning can be put into it, far beyond what Paul was directly thinking of. You young people, in the moments when you are tempted to be impatient of hampering claims, have you ever thought of the price your parents have paid for the blessings you possess? There is hardly anything more heroic in the annals of Scotland than the long unwritten story of the almost incredible sacrifices parents have made to give their sons a university education: and a public authority was saying the other day that it is still happening. Doesn't that make our privileges look a little different?

But it isn't only your parents. Have you ever thought of the price that is being paid for your comforts by the grimy toil of millions of labouring people, whose horny hands and uncultivated minds you would despise? Here is an illustration of it which I owe to Arnold Bennett, the novelist of the Potteries. If you have ever wandered through that Pottery district of Staffordshire, with its industrial towns of Hanley, Burslem, Tunstall, Stoke-on-Trent, Newcastle-under-Lyme, you have perhaps looked with a contemptuous eye on all their squalid ugliness, their coarse depressing industrial grime. Why all this grime? Why can't they wash and be clean, like other places? Well, I'll tell you why. It is because they are manufacturing the baths and wash-hand basins that keep the rest of Britain clean. They pay the price. These towns are grimy and ugly in order that St. Andrews may be clean and beautiful. Doesn't that shed a new light on the comfort of our lives? It is bought with a price.

So is everything else in our lives. You who come to study in this University know very well that your lines have fallen in pleasant places. I've never heard any people anywhere talk of their University and their University town with such relish and delight as you do, and I don't wonder. But do you sometimes wonder at the golden privilege of it all, and think (as on this Founder's Day) of where it has all come from; of those who first lighted a torch of knowledge in this place: and of all the generations that have built up, sometimes at great sacrifice and with austere devotion, the traditions that you so easily inherit? Do the sainted ghosts of the past sometimes step out among these venerable buildings, and make you ashamed of your irresponsibility and selfishness?

Here we are on this quiet Sunday morning, worshipping God in this beloved chapel, in peace and freedom. It is so easy, so familiar, we take it all for granted, as something which could never be threatened—though it is being threatened at this very moment in some Christian countries of Europe, where the days of persecution and martyrdom for Christ have come back again after many centuries. As for us, where did we get these familiar blessings of peace and freedom in the truth? Who paid the price? Well, for example, four hundred and eight years ago yesterday, a few yards from this spot, a young man was burnt to death at the stake —Patrick Hamilton—because he loved truth more than life itself. And with that our minds begin to travel back, through the centuries, over the lands, Scotland and England, France and Germany, Geneva and Rome, and further back, Greece and Egypt and Palestine, each with a great multitude which no man can number of Christian men and women who paid a price for the blessings we possess: the noble army of martyrs, the glorious company of the apostles; and then, at the beginning, Jesus Christ our Lord, moving on at this season

49

of the year with his face stedfastly set to go to Jerusalem, and finally, on a spring morning, giving up His life by crucifixion. That was the price He paid. That is what St. Paul is especially thinking of in this place. Without that, we should not be here at all this morning. We should have nothing to sing about or pray about or preach about. And we believe with St. Paul that somehow this was the manifestation of the sacrificial love of God Himself—somehow it is God Himself that has paid the ultimate price for the blessings of our life and our salvation. If our religion means anything at all, today in chapel, it means that.

How then can we ever again say in our hearts: 'My life is my own, and I can do what I like with my own'? That philosophy of life is now torn to pieces, there isn't a shred of it left to cover the nakedness of our ugly individualism. You'd be ashamed to mention it now; because you are not your own, you are bought with a price.

So we come to the third clause: the practical conclusion.

(3) '*Therefore glorify God.*' It doesn't mean simply 'give thanks to God'; though sheer gratitude is indeed a vital part of any decent life, not to say a Christian life, and when youth is ungrateful, it is one of the ugliest things in the world. But to glorify God, in the historic sense of that noble phrase, means to live one's life for God's glory; and that includes everything most worth living for—the love of God and man, heroism and pity, self-forgetful burden-bearing, the service of God's Kingdom among mankind, everything that lifts our life above the level of self and the flesh and the world, and makes it a brave dedicated thing, a crusade for the Kingdom of Heaven.

Friends, in every place, in every university, in every community, of young or old, there are some who regard their lives in the one way, and some who regard their lives in the other. Some who will never pull their weight, but always be selfish passengers, and others who will always put their backs into the heaviest of the pulling. Some who are always getters only, and others who really believe with Jesus that it is more blessed to give than to get. Some who, even as regards communal activities, will only do the popular things, the jobs that bring applause; and others who are too generous-hearted to think of popularity—they will make themselves of no reputation and do even the unpopular things, if they see a thing that needs to be done for the common good and the glory of God. Some who, even if they profess to be Christians, are terribly safe and discreet about their Christianity, never letting it run away with them, but trying to make the best of both worlds; and others who are not ashamed of the Gospel of Christ or afraid to commit their lives to it.

So it is at any University. So it will be in the world at large when you go down. Some will glorify themselves: and some will glorify God. I put it to you today: which will you do? Jesus Christ, puts it to you today, Jesus Christ the Son of man, who came not to be served but to serve, and to give His life a ransom for many. Have you learnt that you don't belong to yourself, that you have been bought with a price? If so, you will want to glorify God. And you will thank God today with all your heart that you have some gifts which you can pour out, with joy, in the service of His everlasting Kingdom.

Now unto Him that loved us, and hath loosed us from our sins in His own blood, and hath made us to be kings and priests to His God and Father: to Him be glory and dominion for ever and ever. AMEN.

5. IMMORTALITY

He is not the God of the dead, but the God of the living.
MARK 12.27

I WANT to ask the question: Why do we Christians believe in a life after death? What is the Christian argument for immortality?

That may seem indeed a strange subject to choose for a sermon to a youthful student congregation. In the days of youth, death seems very far away, and the question of what lies beyond it seems remote and unimportant. That is true at least in ages of tranquillity and peace. But in the times through which you and I have lived and are still living, life has once more become hazardous and uncertain. Death has been stalking across the world, and has been a frequent visitor not only to old age but to youth; and there have been many things to remind us that 'here we have no continuing city', and that nothing is more characteristic of our human situation than the brevity of life and the certainty of death. Therefore a great many people are again asking the old question: If a man die, shall he live again? Do I really believe in a life beyond the grave? And why?

What is the Christian answer to that question? You may say that we believe in the future life because the New Testament teaches it. Yes, but how does the New Testament know? Those men who wrote the New Testament, those early followers of Christ, why did they believe in a life beyond? They were quite sure of it. They had no doubts. What was the secret? What made them so sure? What was their argument—what is the Christian argument—for immortality?

To begin with: Was it a matter of proving the immortality of the soul, either by a theoretical argument or by a practical experiment? No, I am quite sure it was not. And I want to begin with that negative side.

The ancient Greek philosophers, Socrates and Plato, tried to prove the immortality of the soul by a philosophical argument—by showing that, while the body dies, the soul could not possibly come to an end of its existence, but from its very nature and essence is bound to last on for ever. Those men, Socrates and Plato, were indeed noble souls themselves, with a genuine faith in the life beyond. But I am sure that their faith was something better and deeper than all their arguments. For, after all, suppose you could prove by an absolutely watertight philosophical argument that the soul continues to exist when the body dies—is that of much use in itself? Is it enough? Is it even relevant? Does it tell you what you really want and need to know? Has it anything to do with the Christian hope of eternal life? I do not think it has; and this Christian hope is not something that you can ever prove by a speculative argument.

But then again, people have also tried to prove it by what we may call practical experiment—I mean, by psychical research, and particularly in the name of spiritualism. And I believe that is even further off the track, this dabbling in spiritualism as a religion. It is a very ancient business, but there has been a revival of it in our time. Many people who, in the course of two world wars, lost their friends by death found themselves pining for some certainty about the life beyond, and perhaps did not find the Christian Church giving them a very clear and sure message about it. So in their grief they turned to the spiritualists, consulted mediums, attended séances, and so tried to get into touch with their departed friends and to get messages from the other side. Well, I am not going to make any pronouncement upon the evidence and how it is to be explained. I have not studied it enough for that. I am taking an entirely different line. I want to ask: Even if some of the evidence is honest and genuine and raises curious questions, what is it worth from the point of view of the religious life or the Christian faith? And my answer is: Nothing at all. You know the kind of messages usually reported by the mediums, how unspeakably trivial and commonplace they are. Even if they did prove something about the souls of the dead living on somewhere —is that kind of thing in itself worth proving? Does it tell us anything of what we really need to know? Has it anything to do with our deepest questionings about the purpose of God in time and in eternity? I don't think it has. It is a delusive substitute, when it is made into a religion. And it has nothing to do with the eternal life which we find as the gift of God in the New Testament.

But what then is the basis of our Christian belief in immortality? I will answer that question by saying that it is *faith in God through Jesus Christ.* And now, lest that answer should seem to be a mere escape, I want to work it out in the light of this passage of our text.

In this passage we find Jesus in controversy with the Sadducees on the whole question of a future life, or, as they would put it, the resurrection of the dead. At that time among the Jews it was not yet a regular part of orthodox belief. Some sects, such as the Pharisees, believed in it. But others, like the Sadducees, did not. In this place the Saddu-cees are having an argument with Jesus about it, and they are trying to corner Him, because they know that He believes in it. They put to Him what was meant to be an awkward question, a poser. Jesus disposes of their question; and then He comes to His own positive argument about immortality.

He begins by quoting the Old Testament story about God

54

speaking to Moses out of the Burning Bush. They all knew the story, and had perhaps marvelled at it as a miracle-story, but they had never thought very deeply about what it meant. But now Jesus says to these Sadducees: 'As regards the resurrection of the dead, have you never heard the story of how God spoke from the bush to Moses and said, I am the God of Abraham and of Isaac and of Jacob? He is not the God of the dead, but the God of the living.' You see what Jesus meant. Abraham and Isaac and Jacob were dead and buried long ago at the time when Moses lived. And yet God says: 'I am the God of Abraham and Isaac and Jacob.' How could that be? Is God the God of dead men? A poor kind of God that would be, if He can't save His people from death, if He is content to be called by the names of men who are just dead and done with. Nay, that would not be God at all. God is not like that. He is not the God of the dead, but of the living. And·if He is the God of Abraham and Isaac and Jacob—if they are His men and He is their God—then these men can't be just finally dead. Of course they died and were buried. But that can't be the end of the story. These men must be alive somehow, somewhere, and in God's keeping, in this universe of God's. Therefore there is a resurrection of the dead, there is a life beyond the grave, a real blessed eternal life for God's people; because God is not the God of the dead, but the God of the living.

That was our Lord's argument. I wonder whether you have ever noticed that we find exactly the same argument used, in connection with the very same men, Abraham and Isaac and Jacob, in the eleventh chapter of the Epistle to the Hebrews. These men (says the writer) lived and died in faith, always seeking something that lay ahead, and going out as pilgrims to find it, though they hardly knew what or where it was. But God knew, and He had it ready for them, an eternal city beyond this present life, waiting for them on the other side of death. 'Wherefore,' says the writer, 'God is not ashamed to be called their God: for He hath prepared for them a city.' If He hadn't had any such eternal life prepared for them, He would have been ashamed to be called their God, for He would be the God of dead men, who had let His people down, though they had trusted in Him. But God is not like that. He is not the God of the dead, but the God of the living. And so we may be sure that all who have Him as their God will have the gift of eternal life. A real man of God cannot finally die. A life that is united to God cannot be snuffed out by death.

I am sure that many a perplexed and doubting soul has found that argument of faith rising up in his heart, perhaps unexpectedly, in a time of sore and sudden bereavement—probably some of you here today. Perhaps you never very deeply and consciously believed in a life beyond the grave, perhaps it never really came home to you—until some heavy bereavement came upon you, the death of some noble soul who had been to you as an Abraham, an Isaac or a Jacob. But then suddenly you knew. You realized that you were quite sure. And it was not mere wishful thinking. Nor was it based on any ordinary kind of proof. It was because you believed in God. Because of God, because of His great purpose of redemption, you were quite sure that your departed friend, who was also a friend of God's, could not really be snuffed out by death in this universe of God's. You were quite sure that he was alive—more alive than ever. One of my old theological teachers in Edinburgh gives us a testimony of that kind in one of his letters, written after the sudden death of a greatly honoured friend. This is what he wrote: 'I am so grateful for the vivid belief that I have in his immortality. For some time I have been anxious to have a long and intimate talk with him about some of the perplexities of eternal life.... And now this is the answer: not his suggestions or reasonings, but himself.'

That rings true to life. His friend's death made immortality far more real to him than it was before; and of course it was because he not only knew his friend but also knew God. It is just the same argument from God to immortality.

And now let me bring all this to a climax by coming to the heart of the argument, which is—the supreme case of Jesus Christ Himself. Do you see? To put it at its very least (and this is an understatement): Jesus became the supreme instance, the crucial instance, of His own argument, which clinched it for ever, and made eternal life a surer thing for His people than it had ever been for anybody before. I have been speaking of the argument Jesus used in the words of our text about the life beyond. But that argument never quite came home to his followers until He passed through the gates of death Himself. And then He Himself became the living example of His argument—as we find all over the New Testament.

Let us try to imagine what it meant to those men. They had known Jesus in the flesh, had rubbed shoulders with Him, tramped the roads of Galilee with Him, and been His disciples and friends; and that was far and away the most marvellous experience they had ever had. He had made life a new and wonderful thing to them. He was the light of their lives. And then—Jesus was arrested, and condemned to death, He was crucified, He died, and was buried, and that was the end. Was that the end? Was Jesus really dead? Had death really made an end of Him? A thousand times NO. God had brought him through the jaws of death, and He was alive for ever more. I do not know how that happened. I do not know what exactly it was that took place on that first Easter morning. And if you had asked the disciples, perhaps they could not have answered all your questions either. But they were quite sure that God had brought their

Master through the gates of death, and raised Him up alive. Death had not made an end of Him, but He had somehow made an end of death, as an enemy. Yes, through Jesus Christ death had become a different thing from what it ever was before. He Himself had become the supreme argument for immortality. And now His followers need no longer speak of the God of Abraham and Isaac and Jacob: they can do better still, they can talk of the God of Jesus Christ.

So they said: 'Blessed be the God and Father of our Lord Jesus Christ, who hath begotten us again to a living hope by the resurrection of Jesus Christ from the dead.' They said: 'He that raised up the Lord Jesus will raise us up also with Jesus.' And they spoke of their Master as 'the Lord Jesus Christ, who hath abolished death, and brought life and immortality to light through the Gospel.'

That, in the last analysis, is why Christians believe in eternal life beyond the grave. It is an argument of faith in God through Jesus Christ.

And now one practical word to close with. If that is the Christian argument for immortality, it all depends on our becoming united with God in this present life. In this present world, every day, some people are living the merely temporal life, and others are living the eternal. As you do your work in the world tomorrow, in class or study or laboratory, in shop or factory or office or home, you may have on one side of you a man or woman who is living the merely temporal life, and on the other side, doing just the same work, another who is living the eternal, in faith and obedience, in the knowledge and love of God.

Which life are you living? The kind of life that passes away into nothingness, with the world and its lusts, or the kind that endures for ever because it is united with God?

6. INTELLIGENT CHRISTIANITY

*Be ready always to give an answer to every man that asketh you a
reason of the hope that is in you.* I PETER 3.15

THIS text makes me think of a poem by Thomas Hardy, in
which he describes how, in the twilight of a dreary winter
afternoon he heard a thrush on a branch above his head
suddenly breaking into ecstatic song. Everything around
was so depressing, and there seemed so little visible cause for
such joyful carollings, that Hardy says, in the last verse of
the poem:

> I could but think there trembled through
> His happy good-night air
> Some blessed hope of which he knew
> And I was unaware.

Some blessed hope of which the bird knew and the sad
sceptical pagan poet was unaware. That was Hardy's fancy.

Now that is a very good parable of the situation of which
our text speaks. The text gives us a picture of a sad pagan
world nineteen centuries ago, in which the Christians were
the only people who had a definitely hopeful outlook; so
that the pagans around noticed it and were surprised at it,
as Hardy was at the singing thrush; and they would turn to
the Christians and ask questions about what it was that made
them hopeful. 'Be ready', says Peter, 'to give an answer to
everybody who asks you for a reason of the hope that is in
you.'

I wonder how far Christianity can live up to that in the
world of today. There is plenty of darkness and plenty of
despair. There are plenty of people asking wistfully where
they can get light upon the terrible problems of our age.

And no wonder. But if we are Christians we must believe that Christianity has the answer to the problems. And I am sure that in certain quarters Christianity is facing the issues, thinking them out and giving a hopeful lead in a hopeless world. But how far is *our* Christianity sharing in that lead, or even conveying to the world any impression of possessing a faith and hope that we can hold on to? A great deal of our common Christianity is not live enough for that, and not intelligent enough.

And what I really wish to do this morning is to make a plea for a more intelligent Christianity, a Christianity that has to some extent thought itself out, and knows what it means and believes, and can give some answer to the world's pathetic questions. That is quite especially what this text speaks of—not only the hope that was in the hearts of Christians, but the fact that there was a reason for the hope, and that Christians ought to be able to state it. It is a very curious thing, which has often been pointed out by scholars, that in ancient Greek literature hope is not regarded as a good thing, but as a bad thing, a snare and a delusion, preventing people from facing the facts. But to the early Christians, as you can see in the New Testament, hope was a thing with solid foundations. It had its reasons, and Christians ought to know the reasons. 'Be ready', says Peter, 'to give an answer to everybody who asks you for a reason of the hope that is in you.'

And so I want to make a plea for a more intelligent Christianity.

A friend of mine once said to me that he knew some business men who were at the same time loyal churchmen: in business they were wide awake, keen, competent, powerful; but in their religion they had never got beyond the Sunday School stage. They had never grown up religiously. They had never put a man's mind into their religion. In their religion they still possessed, not the child-like heart, which is a very good thing, but the childish mind and out-look, which is a very different thing and a very poor thing for a grown up man or woman. But isn't that a fairly common case?

I have often wondered why people who are accustomed to reading don't read more books on religious subjects. I mean, people who do otherwise take their Christianity seriously. They are Christians, and they are thinking people generally, they try to keep abreast of the best books as they appear. But they seldom read a book about the great realities of religion, in which they profess to believe: about the meaning of our belief in God, and Providence, and Prayer, and Christ, and the life to come; and about the Bible and all the new light that has been shed upon it in the modern world. And for that matter, they have never taken the trouble to study and understand the Bible itself, with the robust mind of a man. In fact, they are not taking their religion intelligently.

And the result often is that they are ready to be carried away by the queerest winds of doctrine, the craziest religious movements. They can't discriminate because they haven't been thinking of the meaning of what they profess to believe. They may have loved God with their hearts, but they never loved Him with their minds. They never put their minds into their religion. And what a pity! How unworthy of the true spirit of Christianity!

Do you remember what Jesus said to His disciples when He sent them out? 'Behold, I send you forth as sheep in the midst of wolves: be ye therefore wise as serpents, and harmless as doves.' You see, He did not mean His followers to live a sheltered kind of life, as sheep in the fold, protected from all the winds of opinion, safe within high walls, where they could ruminate at peace. No, they were to go out into the world, they were to live among men with all sorts of different opinions; and they must be men too: hard-headed, intelligent, wide-awake, knowing what they believed, able to give an account of themselves and their faith. Not indeed proud and sophisticated—nay, they were to be 'harmless as doves'. But they were also to be 'wise as serpents', Jesus said. They would need it all in this world, and the cause of His Gospel would need it all too.

And you remember how St. Paul once put it, in writing to the Christians at Corinth. 'Brethren, be not children in understanding. In malice be ye children; but in understanding be ye men.' As much as to say: 'Don't imagine that the child-like heart commended by Jesus Christ means the childish mind. No, you must put a man's intelligence into your Christianity.' Remember that Paul was talking to a very mixed group, very few of them really educated, and many of them actually slaves. 'Not many wise. . . .' But they had become Christians, and so they must become intelligent in their faith. Some of them were in danger (Paul saw) of being carried away into a merely emotional type of religion, and Paul tells them that is not good enough for Christians. They must put their mature minds into their Christianity. 'I will pray with the spirit, and I will pray with the understanding also.' 'Brethren, be not children in your understanding: be children as regards malice, but in understanding be men.'

And says Peter: 'Be ready to give an answer to everybody who asks you for a reason of the hope that is in you.' That intelligent kind of Christianity was *expected* of Christians.

Let me give two illustrations, from two very different periods, of how Christians have risen to that demand.

(1) The first is from the early centuries when Christianity went out and conquered the world. Dr T. R. Glover, who was such an authority on that period, tells us that one reason

why Christianity conquered the world was because it did better thinking than the rest of the world. It not only knew better how to live and how to die: it also knew better how to think. It 'out-thought' the world. Here is a deeply interesting passage:

> The Christian read the best books, assimilated them, and lived the freest intellectual life the world had. Jesus had set him to be true to fact.
>
> There is no place for an ignorant Christian. From the very start every Christian had to know and to understand, and he had to read the Gospels, he had to be able to give a reason for his faith.
>
> They read about Jesus, and they knew him, and they knew where they stood. . . . Who did the thinking in that ancient world? Again and again it was the Christian. He out-thought the world.

That does not mean that Christianity was not a religion for ordinary unlearned people. On the contrary, it brought personal religion to the rank and file of humanity, individually, more than had ever been done before. But, you see, Christianity took ordinary folk and made men of them even intellectually—put them on their mettle, and made them intelligent in their faith.

(2) My other example is from our own Scottish Christianity. It has always tried to be an instructed and intelligent Christianity. There is a charming story of a thing that happened in Edinburgh two generations ago, during the visit of the great American evangelist D. L. Moody. One Sunday Moody was conducting a service for children in a large hall packed with Edinburgh boys and girls, and the subject of his address was Prayer. He began with the words: 'What is prayer?', not expecting, of course, any answer. No sooner had he uttered the question than a hundred little hands shot up all over the hall. Moody was astonished, but he picked out one little fellow and asked him for his answer. Without any hesitation the boy stood up and said: 'Prayer is an offering up of our desires unto God, for things agreeable

to His will, in the name of Christ, with confession of our sins and thankful acknowledgment of His mercies.' It was from the Shorter Catechism; and all the others could have said it too. Moody said: 'Thank God, my boy, that you were born in Scotland.'

I'm not suggesting that the Shorter Catechism is a good book for teaching children. But I do like that story because it illustrates how in Scotland people have been accustomed to feeding their religion on strong meat. Too strong, no doubt, when they were children. No doubt Scotland has sometimes in the past made the mistake of treating its children as if they were grown men, in its religious teaching. But that is nothing like as bad as the opposite mistake of treating its grown men as children, or treating ourselves as children, in our religion.

However, I do not wish to sentimentalize about Scotland, but to ask: Are we in Scotland living up to that great tradition? Have you really grown up in your religion? Are you putting the mind of a full-grown man into your Christianity? Or are you leaving it at the infantile stage? What a sad business that would be—especially in this age of change and testing, in which old beliefs are being questioned all around us! Yes, today the world is asking questions, about religion, and there is more need than ever that we who are Christians should love the Lord our God not only with our hearts but with our minds, and be able to represent our Master with full conviction and with intelligent faith.

But now one word more, to avoid misunderstanding. Don't imagine that I mean that in these great matters the mind, so to speak, can ever take the place of the heart, or that you can ever be ready to give a reason of the hope that is in you unless you really have got it in you, the root of the matter, deep down in your heart and life. In this verse Peter is not thinking of the theoretical arguments that can be spun

64

out in an arm-chair and given forth in a jaunty voice. Let us come back and see what he says. 'Sanctify Christ as Lord, in your hearts, and be ready always to give an answer to anyone who asks you for a reason of the hope that is in you.' And then he adds, 'but with humility and reverence, having a good conscience.' It goes as deep as that, involving a commitment of heart and will and conscience. You must love the Lord your God with all your heart and soul and strength.

Yes; but if you do, you will want to love Him with your mind also. You will think much and often of what you believe, that you may know the Gospel and never be ashamed of it, but be able, with both heart and mind, to give a reason for the hope that is in you.

7. THE COMMUNITY OF THE HOLY SPIRIT

And all that believed were together, and had all things in common; and they sold their possessions and goods, and distributed them to all, as any man had need. And day by day, continuing stedfastly in the temple, and breaking bread at home, they took their food with gladness and singleness of heart, praising God, and having favour with all the people. And the Lord added to them day by day those who were being saved.

ACTS 2.44-47

Is Christianity an individual Gospel or a social Gospel? Is it a matter of 'my soul and God', or is it concerned with the social and political order? Wherever I go just now I find that question being asked. and indeed hotly debated, with two opposite answers given. On the one hand I am told that a Christian's primary concern is with the salvation of his own soul in preparation for the world to come, and that the Church ought not to be directly interested in social or economic reform, because the real evil is the moral and spiritual evil in men's hearts, and it can only be dealt with by individual conversion. So true Christianity is an individual Gospel. Well, that sounds pretty deep. But then, on the other hand, I am told that true Christianity is a social Gospel, with a programme for the transformation of human society and a passion to make this world a better place for all sorts and conditions of men. Therefore, the Christian Church can't possibly stand aside from the social evils and problems of the age. It dare not keep silent about them, its message must be vitally concerned with them. And as for the individual, if he is more interested in saving his own soul than in securing social justice and opportunity for his less fortunate fellows, his religion is a religion of selfish escape, whereas true Christianity is a social Gospel.

66

These are the two sides of it, and they are constantly put up against each other in these days. On the one hand: 'What's the good of a social Gospel if our individual souls have not been saved?' And on the other hand: 'What's the good of an evangelical Christianity that doesn't deal with social evils?' Well, which of these is right? Is true Christianity an individual or a social Gospel? Does it speak to us of an individual salvation, or of a new social order?

Surely the right answer is 'Both'. And both together. They can't be separated, or they both go bad. I want to try to show that, with the aid of this story which all the Christian world is pondering on this Whitsunday—the story of Pentecost.

If you had been present as a sympathetic stranger in the city of Jerusalem on that Day of Pentecost, you would have been struck by two things. First, you would have been struck by the way in which all sorts of ordinary people had all at once come to have a personal religion of their own. In the ancient world, religion was much more a public matter than a personal matter, and the rank and file of humanity were hardly expected to have a personal knowledge of God. They were expected to take their religion on trust, at second hand, as decent citizens. Of course there were outstanding people, choice spirits, on whom God poured out His Spirit, and they became seers or prophets; they were very exceptional. They knew God directly. But now, you would have said on the Day of Pentecost, that seems to be happening to all sorts of people. They are coming to know God for themselves. Well, that is just what was happening. That was just what you'd have heard Simon Peter say in his speech. He said: 'This is what was predicted by the prophet Joel—It shall come to pass in those days, saith the Lord, that I will pour out of my spirit upon all flesh; and your sons and your daughters shall be like prophets, and your young men shall see visions, and your old men shall dream dreams; and even on my servants and on my handmaidens I will pour out of my spirit.' The fact is: the Gospel of Jesus had made religion a far more personal thing, for the ordinary individual, than it had ever been before, and it was on the Day of Pentecost that this came home to them. You'd have seen it quite plainly.

But if you had been there, you would also have been struck by another thing (here is the paradox). You would have noticed that religion had also, all at once, become a more deeply social thing than it had ever been before. Quite plainly, this was not any lone-wolf kind of religion. There was nothing solitary, or introverted, or cloistered, or escapist, about it. It was extraordinarily communal. These people— all sorts and conditions of men and women—seemed to have become a new community, with one heart and one soul, with a new and wonderful comradeship that the world had never seen before. Quite true. The like of it had never been seen. And it was not mere emotion and sentiment. It was practical, and sacrificial. These people would do anything for each other—they even forgot all about the rights of private property, and made a little experiment in voluntary communism in Jerusalem. There sprang up a new kind of care for the poor, and presently a new attitude to slaves. They had a new sense of loyal responsibility for all their fellow-creatures, and they started to spread the good thing that had made them into a community. Of course they didn't embark upon a programme of social reform. They didn't even try to banish slavery. How could they? They had no political power in the great Roman Empire; most of them had no vote; they had none of the opportunities of modern democracy—that was far beyond the horizon. But the spirit was there—a spirit of community with all mankind—a new community without distinctions of class or race, in which every man was a child of God, a slave just as much as his master. *That was Christianity.*

Yes, and that is still true Christianity. And now that we do live in an age of democracy, where we all have voting power, and must all share responsibility for the dreadful evils of our social system, the Christianity that did not care about social reform would not be genuine Christianity at all.

There is an old Indian Buddhist story, which I believe has often been told in Christian pulpits, about a wise king who undertook to teach a young man the secret of spiritual freedom. This was how he did it. The young man was to be given a jar filled with oil to the very brim, and he was to carry it through the streets of the town, where a fair was going on, without spilling a drop. An executioner, with drawn sword, was ordered to walk behind him, and upon the first drop of oil being spilt, was to strike off the young man's head. The young fellow agreed, did what he was told, and carried the jar safely back to the king without having lost a drop. The king asked him: 'As you walked through the town, whom and what did you see?' 'Sir,' said the young man, 'I kept my eyes fixed on the vessel of oil, and saw and heard nothing else.' And then the king told him that such was the secret of spiritual freedom: to be so intent on keeping one's own soul that one was blind to the affairs of one's fellows.

It is a good story. But that is a Buddhist parable of spiritual freedom. And now, for contrast, take the Christian picture. It comes just after the story of Pentecost, and the people of whom it speaks are the people who had had that deep personal experience of the Holy Spirit of God, searching out the depths of their individual souls. But this is how it showed to the world: 'And all those who believed had all things in common, and they sold their possessions and goods, and distributed them to all, as anybody had need. And day by day, continuing stedfastly in the temple, with one accord, and breaking bread in private houses, they took their food with gladness and singleness of heart, praising God, and having favour with all the people. And the Lord added to them daily such as were being saved.'

'Being saved': What does that mean? It does not mean a passport for a place called heaven. It means being transformed into the sort of person that can't separate his own welfare from that of his fellows—that can't bear to see his fellow-creatures missing the true opportunities of life, or living in conditions he wouldn't live in himself. But doesn't salvation mean being set free from my sins? Yes, and sin is equal to self-centredness, and my supreme sin is that I don't care enough about the welfare and the woes of my fellows, both spiritual and material. Perhaps my greatest sin is that when there were three millions of unemployed folk in this country, and hundreds of thousands of youths being ruined by it in body and soul, I didn't care anything like enough about it. And if we don't care enough yet, and if, when that kind of problem comes again, we haven't cared enough to find a way out—we Christians—that will indeed be the day of judgment for the Church of Christ, showing that it has substituted self-centred sentimentalism for the Pentecostal spirit of community.

Now let me not be misunderstood. I do not for one moment mean that the Christian Church or pulpit should preach political programmes. But it ought to denounce social evils, and it ought to stab awake the consciences of its members about the great sin of their social callousness. Again: I do not suggest that everyone who shouts slogans of social reform is near the Kingdom of God or the Gospel of Christ. It is quite easy to make that kind of thing an escape from God and from Christ. It is dreadfully easy, especially if we have some discontents of our own, to shout slogans

70

about a new social order, and even to get fussy and busy about social reform, without really caring a scrap about our fellows—without one drop in our hearts of the milk of human kindness, not to mention Christian love. That kind of thing may be just a feverish escape from God and our own souls. That's no use. But what I do say is: that when we do hear God's voice through Jesus Christ, it calls us out of ourselves into community with God and man. And then individual Gospel and social Gospel become all one—we can't separate them, without killing both, and running away from God.

So I want to close with one word of appeal, not so much to the people of my generation, but to you young men and women, whose life lies before you. My friend—whoever you are—I don't need to tell you that there is something dreadfully wrong with the world you live in. Also I don't need to tell you that there is something wrong with yourself. And how can you care about getting the world put right for other folk until you have got yourself put right? And yet how can you get yourself put right except by coming to care more for other folk—because what is wrong with you is self-centredness?

That seems a queer tangle. Well, the Gospel of Christ has everything to do with that tangle. God was incarnate in Jesus Christ, and He created in the world a new community —the fellowship of the Holy Spirit—to draw us out of ourselves into community with God and man, for our own salvation and the salvation of the world.

And if you, my friend, feel your heart pierced, in this your day and generation, by the woes of your fellows, that is perhaps the beginning of God's work in your heart, saving you from yourself, drawing you out of yourself, into a life worth living, where you will be lifted above your own temptations and defeats by the enthusiasm of the service of God and man, in the Community of the Holy Spirit.

If God is beginning that work in you—let Him have His way.

8. THE DOCTRINE OF THE TRINITY

In the name of the Father, and of the Son, and of the Holy Ghost.
                                                    MATTHEW 28.19

ON this Trinity Sunday I wish to speak about the doctrine of the Trinity. That sounds formidable and uninviting. But surely we ought not to shirk the task of understanding it. We sing 'God in three Persons, blessed Trinity.' What do we mean? Perhaps we couldn't say. Perhaps we are just mystified. Perhaps this doctrine of three in one, of Trinity in Unity, conveys nothing to our minds but the sense of sheer mystery.

Well, even that is something. The sense of mystery is quite wholesome, in all our thoughts of God, for no human mind can comprehend Him. But mystery is not enough. We need a positive Gospel. And I believe we can find the whole Christian Gospel summed up in this mysterious doctrine, of three Persons, Father, Son and Holy Spirit, in one God. Let us try.

(1) First of all: *One God.* That is very important. It is part of the good news. When Christianity first went out into the pagan world with its Gospel, many people were tired of the old religions, and this was one of the really splendid things about the new Gospel: that instead of a whole host of gods it offered them ONE true God. To us that is so familiar that we don't realize what good news it is. But we would realize it if we had been brought up in a religion which had many gods. You can read in missionary books today of how it comes as a tremendous relief to heathen people when they learn from Christian missionaries that, instead of a whole host of gods and spirits to be propitiated, there

is one great God over all, and that they have to do with Him alone.

A famous divine of the middle ages said wittily that the Devil was the first grammarian, when he taught men to give a plural to the word God. It ought not to have a plural. For if you have more than one God, you never know where you are. To put it into modern terms: if you divide your heart between different loyalties, if you idolize many things, if you believe not only in Providence, but also in blind Fate, and in lucky numbers and charms and mascots, and in the Almighty Dollar above all, then life is distracted, your heart is torn asunder, because you have too many gods. Anything more than One is too many. For there is only one true God. That is what the great prophets of Israel told the world, when the world had gone astray after many gods. They said: All that is based on a lie, and a tragic lie, which destroys all justice and truth and trust among men, and turns the universe into a chaos of conflicting forces and claims. It is a lie. And the truth is far better. It is the good news of One God who governs the whole world in righteousness and mercy; and to trust in Him alone is salvation. 'Look unto me and be ye saved, all the ends of the earth. For I am God, and there is none else.'

That was something gained once for all in the education of the human race, and never to be lost or forgotten: the good news that *God is One*. That is fundamental.

Why wasn't that enough? Why did Christianity have to go on to say something more, and something so complicated and mysterious—that in the Unity there is a Trinity? It was not because God, as it were, dropped down from heaven a ready-made doctrine for our acceptance, a mathematical doctrine of three in one and one in three. That is not how God reveals His truth, and if He did, it wouldn't help us much, but would simply leave us guessing. Why then did

Christianity have to go on from the One God to the Three-in-One?

Well, it was because something happened, and then something else happened. There were two new facts of history and experience. Let us think what they were.

(2) *The fact of Jesus Christ.* About nineteen centuries ago there appeared among the Jews in Palestine a new religious leader, a working-man called Jesus. His career did not last long, for He got into trouble with the authorities and was condemned to death. But on His followers He had made such an impression that they were faced with a quite new task of explanation. Who and what was this Jesus? He had come into their lives and made everything different. He had brought God into their lives in a way they had never known before, and He had brought forgiveness and joy and power and victory over sin and death. He had been put to death Himself, yet somehow they were convinced that His very death had been the greatest victory of all, reconciling sinners to God; and to complete the victory, He had risen from the dead.

But how could Jesus accomplish all that? What was the meaning of it? The only possible meaning, they felt, was this: that God was in Christ. This was not just Jesus of Nazareth. Somehow, it was God. Yet how could that be? Was Jesus simply identical with God? Was 'Jesus' just another name for God? No, that could not be quite right. For Jesus was a real Man, in both body and mind. Jesus talked about God, and He used to pray to God; and He was tempted, as all men are, and He suffered pain, and then He died on the Cross. But not one of these things could be said without qualification about God the Father Almighty.

Then was Jesus a kind of second God, alongside of God the Father? No, that was impossible, for there could not be two Gods. God is eternally one. Then was Jesus a kind of demi-god, something between God and Man, half and half? No, that would be of no use, for then you would lose both the divine and the human. Jesus would be neither God nor Man, but a mythological figure, like the demi-gods that were so plentiful in other religions. That was not a bit like the Christ they had known: and what could such a figure do for man's salvation? It was not a demi-god, but the very God Himself, that they needed and that they found in Jesus.

What then were they to say about it? Well, they had to go on and find new expressions, and say things that had never been said about God before. They said that God became incarnate in Jesus; and yet somehow God did not become wholly, absolutely incarnate, for they knew that God also remained all the time the eternal invisible omnipotent God in Heaven. They had to make further distinctions. So they said it was the Word of God that became incarnate. 'The Word was made flesh.' But there was another expression still more natural. Jesus Himself had continually spoken of God as His Father, and He had a deep continual sense of sonship to God. So they began to speak of the Son of God. It was not God the Father, but God the Son, that was incarnate and became Man. They did not mean that there were two Gods, or that God the Father and God the Son were two quite separate individuals like a human father and son, for there can only be one God. Really they meant something they could not adequately put into words at all. For in Jesus Christ something new and tremendous had come into their lives, and it stretched all their thoughts of God to find new expressions. So they came to speak of the Father and the Son; and even if they couldn't quite explain it or think it out, it was at the very heart of their faith.

It was all because of this tremendous new fact in their experience—the fact of Jesus Christ.

(3) *The fact of Pentecost.* But something else happened, and there is another historic fact that went to the making of the doctrine of the Trinity. We may indicate it by the word Pentecost.

Remember that the disciples of Jesus had their Master with them in the flesh for only a few brief years, and that no other Christians ever since have had that experience at all. To the disciples it was an infinitely marvellous experience. Jesus had brought God into their lives. And if they ever faced the thought that He might be taken away from them suddenly, the prospect of such a bereavement was overwhelming. How could they ever get on at all without Him? Their whole faith in God would collapse.

But if a few months after the departure of Jesus you had asked these disciples whether they missed their Master very badly, and whether they had lost God out of their lives altogether, they would have replied with a joyful and unanimous NO. Indeed they would have told you that somehow the Divine Presence was far more real and powerful in their lives now than ever it had been while their Master was with them in the flesh. It was expedient, they now saw, that their Master should have departed in order that this new experience should come to them.

There was one great day in particular when the experience came home to them. It was on the date of a Jewish festival called Pentecost. The disciples and some others who had become Christians were assembled in a large room in Jerusalem for fellowship and prayer, when they had a marvellous experience, an overwhelming sense of the presence and power of God. And now they were quite sure that they had lost neither God nor Jesus. Jesus seemed nearer than ever. Though they could not see Him with their eyes, it was only now that they began really to understand Him. And God had come into their lives as never before—far more marvellously than even while their Master was on earth—so that now they could go anywhere and witness for Him. Moreover, they very soon found that this great experience need not be confined to those who had known Jesus in the flesh. This was a thing that could happen to anybody anywhere, through the story of Jesus. A new power was abroad in the world; and wherever the apostles went with the message, the new thing kept on happening, in the lives of all sorts of people, just as it had come to the apostles themselves on the Day of Pentecost.

What was it? Was it simply the Jesus they had known, now come back to them unseen? Yes, in a way. They did sometimes speak of it as the presence of Christ. And yet it was not just the same. It was something greater and more universal than what they had known when Jesus was with them in the flesh—the same, yet different, deepened and widened and freed from all limitations of space and time. Was it, then, simply the presence of the Eternal God Himself? Yes, and yet it was something new, something beyond what men had ever known of God before, something that could not have happened but for the work of Jesus.

What was it? How were they to define it? Well, they remembered that in the Old Testament, whenever such a power came into the lives of certain outstanding and exceptional men, it was described as the Spirit of the Lord coming upon them. They remembered also that a prophet called Joel had once foretold the coming of a time when the Spirit of God would be poured out, not on a few exceptional people, but on all sorts of ordinary men and women. And they remembered that their own Master Jesus had said God would give His Holy Spirit to those who asked Him. So now on the Day of Pentecost they said: 'This is what Joel predicted. This is what Jesus promised. And God our Heavenly Father, who came to us in His Son Jesus, is with us now, and for evermore, in this new and wonderful way, through His Holy Spirit.'

And that is how Christians have come to speak of Father, Son and Holy Spirit, One God.

Can you see now why I said that the doctrine of the Trinity sums up the whole Christian Gospel? I began by saying that it is good news to learn that God is One. But, as you see, there is still better news in the message that the One God is Father, Son and Holy Spirit, when you really understand it. Of course to say merely 'three in one and one in three'—that in itself means nothing. But when it comes at the end of the story, it tells you everything. It tells you of what God is, in His eternal and infinite love; and of what God did in Jesus Christ for our salvation; and of what God does still today, dwelling with us as truly as He dwelt among men nineteen centuries ago, and the same for evermore. So to those who know the story, the doctrine of the Trinity sums up the whole Gospel. And the Church never tires of singing in gratitude: 'Glory be to the Father, and to the Son, and to the Holy Ghost: as it was in the beginning, is now, and ever shall be, world without end.'

9. THE GLORY OF THE CROSS

Most gladly therefore will I rather glory in my infirmities, that the power of Christ may rest upon me.　　　　　2 CORINTHIANS 12.9

God forbid that I should glory, save in the cross of our Lord Jesus Christ.
　　　　　GALATIANS 6.14

I WANT to begin by quoting to you a question that was once put to me by a layman of my acquaintance. I was telling him the story of a very sad thing that had happened in the life of our College. A young fellow who had come from rather a poor home, but who was doing exceedingly well as a student, was suddenly taken ill in the middle of his course, and after a very short illness he died. His parents, whose pride and joy he was, were left without any children, and with broken hearts. I was in a bus, on my way to visit them, when I met my layman acquaintance. He asked me where I was going, and I told him the sad story. Immediately he said to me: 'Now, was it God that did that, or was it the Devil?' He was not a theologian or a thinker. His question was the naïve straightforward question of a plain man. Perhaps he did not know that he was sounding the very depths of the problem of human existence. He was asking a question which cannot be answered glibly in a single word, but which involves the whole Christian doctrine, not only of divine providence, but of divine redemption.

That is exactly the question which St. Paul wrestles with and answers in this first passage.

St. Paul suffered from some chronic and painful ailment, which even had a certain crippling effect. We do not know what it was, though there have been various theories, but that doesn't matter. In any case it was very troublesome, and persistent, and recurrent. Now, was it God, or was it the Devil, that sent it upon him? The extraordinary thing about this passage is that Paul seems to say that somehow it was both. But he only got to that point by stages, and we must follow the stages.

(1) In the first place, *Paul began by hating his malady*, as every healthy-minded man must hate suffering and disease, whether his own or his neighbour's. And I believe Paul hated it not only because it was painful and unpleasant, but because it hindered his work and so seemed to make him less useful in his great missionary enterprise. He spoke of it as a 'thorn in his flesh', as if it were like a sharp wooden stake being driven into his body with agonizing pain. He even spoke of it as 'the messenger of Satan' (or 'the angel of Satan'). It was the Devil's work, it was brought about by the powers of the kingdom of evil. That reminds us exactly of how we find Jesus in the Gospel story talking of human suffering and disease. It was the work of the Kingdom of Satan, torment-ing human life. And Jesus set Himself to free people from it in the name and by the power of the Kingdom of God. Paul knew all about that. And so he prayed, and prayed again and again, that he might be set free from his painful malady.

That was a very Christian thing to do. But that was not the end of it . That was only the first stage.

(2) The second stage was when *Paul got an answer to his prayer*. But was his prayer answered? Yes, of course it was; and he tells us what the answer was. It was not the answer that he expected or desired. But he never dreamt of repining about it, but the very opposite. This is what he tells us about the ailment and the prayer and the answer. 'Concerning this thing I besought the Lord three times that it might depart from me. And He has said to me, My grace is suffi-cient for you, for my strength is made perfect in weakness.

81

Most gladly therefore will I rather glory in my infirmities, that the power of Christ may rest upon me.' Do you see what that means? Paul discovered through Christ that while suffering is a bad thing in itself, which no sane person would wish to have, yet suffering may help to make better men and women of us, may enrich and beautify our lives, if we face it in the right way. And that does not mean facing it in a spirit of defeatist resignation or hypochondria, but facing it in a spirit of faith and love. Then God's power works through our very infirmity, gives us spiritual strength out of weakness, makes life even a richer nobler thing. That was what Paul came to see, as an answer to his prayer.

And though it sounds so unlikely, isn't it true to life? You and I have seen it too, or will some day see it, if not in our own case, then in the lives of others whom we know. Here is a man (you can think of names for yourselves) whose life has been chequered with trouble and sorrow beyond the common lot. And through it all he has become nobler, finer, braver, kinder, than the people around him; not automatically (for it does not always happen), but by faith and love. That is how, when we can't get rid of our troubles, Christ can utilize them and bring good out of them. Here is a fine sentence by that great Roman Catholic thinker Baron von Hügel: 'Jesus cures pain and disease, as though they could not be utilized, whilst Jesus also trains and empowers souls to utilize their sufferings as though they were incurable.' That possibility of strength out of weakness was what Paul discovered. And that was the second stage.

(3) But there was a third stage; and it seems to reach the height of absurdity. *Paul arrived at the point of being able to say that somehow it was God that even sent the trouble upon him.* In fact, if you look again at the passage, you will find that that is how he begins the whole story. As he looks back, he introduces the whole subject by saying 'There was *given*

82

unto me a thorn in the flesh, the messenger of Satan to buffet me'. 'There was given unto me!' By whom? Of course he means by God. Was it God, or was it the Devil that did this? Paul tells us in the same sentence, in the same breath, that somehow it was both. His troublesome malady was the angel of Satan to buffet him, but it was also the gift of God to make a true man of him. And when Paul said that, wasn't he saying something profoundly true about the tragedies of this our mortal life?

I am not speaking of the question whether you are to believe in a personal devil. It makes no difference at this point of the argument. In any case there is such a thing as evil in the universe, and it is so vast and dreadful that we may well think of it as a Kingdom of Evil fighting against the Kingdom of God. But the worst part of the evil, the fundamental tragedy, is the moral and spiritual evil in which you and I are personally involved. We are sinful selfish men and women, we have gone wrong, we are very far from being the kind of persons God meant us to be. That is what above all needs to be put right. And (don't you see?) that could only be put right in the rough and tumble of a world where we have to suffer pain and sorrow and struggle against them. It is only in such a world, with the discipline of all its hazards and hardships, that human souls can be remade in the image of God. Therefore, how can we stop short of saying that the very hardships are the gifts of God for our salvation? Of course happiness is a good thing, and we all want it and need it; and pain and sorrow are evil things, the tragic marks of a ruined and fallen world. But that is not the whole story. For those very elements of tragedy which come to us as the fruits of the Kingdom of Evil come also as God's instruments of salvation, to save us from the evil, to make us into His true sons and daughters, and to lead us at last into the perfect beatitude of the life everlasting. The messenger of Satan becomes the gift of God in this great Christian Gospel of divine providence and divine redemption.

But now, to complete the argument, let us ask: How did Christianity arrive at that profound way of dealing with the tragedy of the world? The answer to that question is found in the second text I gave you, where Paul says: 'God forbid that I should glory, save in the cross of our Lord Jesus Christ.' What brought things to a head and drove men at last to this great conviction about the ways of God was—the crucifixion of Jesus.

That was the worst thing that ever happened. Men had long been asking questions about the dreadful things that were allowed to happen in this world—things that made people wonder whether there was any meaning at all in human life, or any God in heaven. But now came the most dreadful thing of all, driving the sharp point of the problem deeper into the human heart than it had ever gone before— the crucifixion of Jesus. Was it God that did that, or was it the Devil? Of course it was the Devil and all his hosts: the jealousy of the Pharisees, the scheming of the Sadducees, the treachery of Judas, the hysteria of the crowd; and behind all that, the demonic powers of darkness, which 'crucified the Lord of glory'. The men who wrote the New Testament are quite clear about that. This was a thing that never ought to have happened, the most godless thing that was ever done in this wicked world—the crucifixion of Jesus.

But was that the whole truth? Is that all they had to say about it? No, indeed. All over the New Testament we find this extraordinary conviction; that the crucifixion of Jesus was not only the worst thing that had ever been done through the wickedness of devils or men, but also the best thing that had ever happened in the merciful providence of God. God was in it—not in the sense that God from His throne in heaven appointed this fate for an innocent man called Jesus,

84

but in the sense that God was in Christ, and when He suffered and died on the Cross, this was God Himself bearing the sin and suffering of the world. This was the defeat of evil, this was the victory of divine love, this was the redemption of the world. So that the very word 'Cross', which to ancient ears was as terrible as the word 'gallows' is to us, has become transformed into a symbol of all that is most glorious and divine; and Paul can speak (in words which would seem highly paradoxical if they were not so familiar) of 'glorying' in the gallows, the Cross of Christ.

That is how the Christian doctrine of Providence went so deep and rose so high that it became part of a whole drama of redemption. And Paul was able to say 'Most gladly will I glory in my infirmities, that the power of Christ may rest upon me'—he was able to say that because he had learned to 'glory in the cross of the Lord Jesus Christ'.

And now one word about the question, What has all this to do with us? But it is plain—isn't it?—that this is a good and fit gospel for such a world as ours.

It may indeed be that to some of you young men and women both the thorn in the flesh and the Cross of Christ seem pretty far away and unreal. Perhaps life has not yet very many thorns for you, and your hearts cry out for joy. So you sometimes wonder why Christianity must talk so much about a Cross, why it need put that tragic emblem in the centre. Yes, but sometimes also—and I am sure this happens to many young people today—you have a vision of the countless shameful crosses that are always in the world, the infinite mass of human tragedy and evil, and of your own share in the sinful responsibility for it. Sometimes that sudden vision stabs your heart, like a thorn driven into your flesh. And then you can thank God that Christianity has something to say about it all, that it is not a religion of easy rosy optimism in such a world. You can thank God that this

Christianity which has come down to us is a religion that faced the worst and went down into the depths and endured the Cross before it rose up and proclaimed the victory and the glory in its Gospel.

And now, through that very vision that stabs your heart, He that reigns from the tree stretches out His hands to bless you, to embrace you in His salvation, and to call you to His royal service in this tragic world.

10. REJOICE

Rejoice in the Lord alway; and again I say, Rejoice.
PHILIPPIANS 4.4

THE great Danish thinker of a century ago, Søren Kierke-
gaard, has an extraordinary passage in his *Journal*, about a
man who went mad through continually thinking of the
revolution of the earth upon its axis. He became continu-
ously and morbidly obsessed by the fact, of which we are all
aware, that we are all the time being whirled through space
at an immense velocity; and it got upon his nerves and drove
him mad. That is an extravagant fancy, which of course
could not have occurred to anyone in a pre-Copernican age.
But it makes me think of what is a common spiritual phenomenon in our age—it might indeed be called the predicament
of the age. We are living in an age of storm and stress, in
which we are being whirled through constant change and
peril. Nothing seems stable, nothing 'stays put', world-
shaking events are happening in the most bewilderingly
rapid succession, on every hand, all round the world. We
cannot open a morning's paper or switch on a radio set
without hearing of them. To all except children and utterly
irresponsible persons life seems to be a continual round of
problems and anxieties, and people do sometimes tell themselves that it is enough to drive anybody mad.

Moreover, not only do we become obsessed by these
problems, but sometimes we almost feel that we *ought* to be
obsessed by them; so that our very religion tends to become
a religion of problems and obsessions. There have been ages
when men could live the Christian life in earnest without

very much consciousness of the tragedies of human existence in the wide world. When we read a book like Boswell's *Life of Samuel Johnson*, we seem to enter into a quiet and spacious eighteenth century world in which a deeply Christian soul like Dr Johnson could practise his religion in a realm apart from the great affairs of nations. But no one can draw that line today, and any wide-awake Christian would be ashamed to try to draw it. Our minds are all the time being bombarded, through radio and the newspapers, with news of catastrophic events on every part of the surface of this planet, and it is in that whirlwind that we have to live our Christian lives. So we learn an anxious and burdened habit of mind. Our very religion becomes a religion of problems, and perhaps we sometimes almost feel that we would be ashamed to have a more serene and untroubled sort of religion.

Do you remember the extraordinarily vivid passage in which Nehemiah tells us how he couldn't help being profoundly depressed when he thought of the ruin of his ancestral city of Jerusalem? He himself was living far away at the brilliant court of the king of Persia, a courtier and a favourite, with every comfort and no troubles. But one day he got news that his own beloved far-away city of Jerusalem was in ruins and was going from bad to worse. And a great sadness came upon him, so that he could not even conceal it when he presented the cup to the king at the royal table. One day the king noticed it. 'Wherefore the king said unto me, Why is thy countenance sad, seeing thou art not sick? This is nothing else but sorrow of heart. Then I was very sore afraid, and said unto the king: Let the king live for ever: why should not my countenance be sad, when the city, the place of my fathers' sepulchres, lieth waste, and the gates thereof are consumed with fire?' How exactly that expresses what we sometimes feel amid the evils and tragedies of the world! We can't forget them, and we ought not to forget them; and when we think of them, a spirit of anxiety and depression comes over us. We feel that in such a world any decent man, still more any Christian, is bound to have a sad and burdened heart. 'Why should not my countenance be sad when I think of the woes of the world?' That sounds quite right, and most Christian.

Is it? Is that the whole truth? I want to point out two remarkable facts which I have noticed and which seem to point in a somewhat different direction.

(1) *God's best servants are not sad.* The saddest and most depressed people whom I see around me in the world are not the people who are doing most to relieve the misery of men and to bear the burdens of their fellows. These two things do not seem to go together. I know people who are full of help for everybody, always sheltering some lame duck, always befriending lonely souls, always leading and supporting good causes, and bearing more than their share of the misery of the world, because they can't forget their fellows. But these people are not continually depressed about the tragedy of things. If they were, I don't believe they would have any strength to spare for burden-bearing. But they are happy warriors, glad hearts, joyful spirits, not groaning always about the woes of mankind, but doing things, helping people, with hearts at leisure for sympathy with others, and with a calm courage which is infectious. Their sympathy is not of the sentimental or emotional kind. It lies in the sphere of the will, which is so much more wholesome. After all, it is quite easy for us to indulge in an emotional sympathy which is a substitute for active service. We become tragic, we groan and sigh, but it is an emotional luxury and may even be an escape from costly burden-bearing. It is only God that can carry the burdens of the whole world, and when we tragically profess to be doing it, we are not really bearing anybody's burden, but just adding to the depression.

God's best servants are not like that. They have far deeper sympathy than most of us, they really care about other people, they do not pass by on the other side, they are 'good Samaritans'. But they are not sad souls. They are glad, with a stream of peace and serenity which runs on underneath all the sorrow. These are the real helpers of mankind: 'sorrow- ful, yet always rejoicing; poor, yet making many rich; having nothing, and yet possessing all things.' That is the first of the two things I have noticed.

(2) *The religion of the Bible is a religion of joy.* You get it even long before the coming of Christ, in the Book of Psalms. 'Be glad in the Lord, and rejoice, ye righteous, and shout for joy all ye that are upright in heart.' How often the Psalmists strike that note, sometimes even calling upon the whole of nature to rejoice with them. 'Let the heavens rejoice, and let the earth be glad. Let the sea roar, and the fullness thereof. Let the field be joyful and all that is therein; then shall all the trees of the wood rejoice, before the Lord.' And when you come to the New Testament, you will find that the word 'joy' has become one of the key-words of Christianity, just like 'faith' and 'love' and 'peace'. Christ says to His disciples: 'Your sorrow shall be turned into joy. . . . I will see you again, and your heart shall rejoice, and your joy no man taketh from you.' And in the Acts of the Apostles and in the Epistles we see how that certainly came true. Those men of the New Testament were happy, they were joyful. Joy was one of the marks of the Christian life. When Paul sets out to give a list of the fruits of the Spirit, he mentions love first, as you might expect, and then second he puts this more un- expected thing called joy. Another apostle calls it 'joy un- speakable and full of glory'. And here in our text Paul says to his fellow-Christians at Philippi: 'Rejoice in the Lord alway; and again I say, Rejoice.' That is the Christianity of the New Testament. It is a religion of joy.

It is not that these people were living in a prosperous and tranquil age and in highly favourable circumstances, or that they went about this tragic world in blinkers because they were wholly intent upon the joys of the next. Far from it. It is quite extraordinary how often we find those men of the Bible saying that they were living in bad times and in an evil world. Often they themselves were living hard and persecuted lives. The Apostle Paul, who wrote these words about rejoicing, was a hunted and homeless man, and he had a profound sense of the wickedness of the world, the moral corruption of human society, whether Jewish or Gentile. Moreover, he could not shrug his shoulders and wash his hands of it all. He had to throw himself right into the middle of the tragic mess. And that meant burden-bearing, anxiety, and sometimes bitter suffering, grief and shame. 'For thy sake we are killed all the day long; we are accounted as sheep for the slaughter.' Sometimes, of course, he was troubled and cast down. 'Without were fightings, within were fears.' And yet, underneath all that there was a deep constant current of gladness, and that is the authentic original Christianity of the New Testament. 'Rejoice in the Lord alway; and again I say, Rejoice.'

(3) So we must ask finally: *What was the secret of it?* How was it possible, and how is it possible, for wide-awake responsible sympathetic warm-hearted people to be as happy as that amid the woes and sorrows of the world? How can a man keep facing all these facts and bearing all these burdens among his fellows, and yet keep on rejoicing?

The answer is: A man can do it when he believes in the purpose of God and the victory of God. That is the secret. That is how it was with the men of the New Testament. They had that sure and certain hope, and they were exhilarated by it. No doubt they expected things to happen in a way in which they did not happen: they thought that Christ would come back to earth very soon and make an end of all the misery and set up His Kingdom, and things did not happen just like that. But the substance of what they believed was just what we believe if we are Christians: that God has a splendid purpose which He is working out through all the confusion of earth, and it runs out beyond this earthly scene altogether into the unseen and eternal, and it is splendid enough to make everything worth while. God has purposes for the human race which run out into all eternity, and they are full of glory. God has purposes for the individual men and women that make up the human race, gracious purposes that reach out beyond life and death into realms unknown beyond the grave and into the ages of eternity. The chequered life of sorrow and suffering that we see on this earthly scene is only a tiny fragment of a magnificent drama that stretches out through death and beyond all our imagination. And the plot of the drama is so splendid, and its climax so wonderful, that Paul can say: 'I reckon that the sufferings of this present time are not worthy to be compared with the glory that is going to be revealed to us; . . . because the creation itself will be set free from the bondage of decay, to obtain the glorious liberty of the sons of God.' That is what God is doing with us, and making of us. That is the plot of the story. That is what it is leading to, at the last, in the great purpose of God.

How do we know? Because of what God has done already in Jesus Christ. That is the central chapter of the story, and it gives us the plot, and it is a good one, and it leads to a more joyful ending than we could ask or think. When we believe that, then we become part of the plot, and God makes use of us in working it out, and we can enjoy it, even when it is costly; and then God can use us all the better, as His happy warriors.

Therefore: 'Rejoice in the Lord alway; and again I say, Rejoice.'

O Heavenly Father, we beseech Thee to forgive us that we hide from Thee so much and trust Thee so little. Grant us a vision of Thy purpose of love, that our hearts may rejoice because we have trusted in Thy holy Name. And so grant that Thy joy may be our strength in the service of Thy Kingdom. Through Jesus Christ our Lord.

11. CONVERSION OF ST. PAUL

When it pleased God, who separated me from my mother's womb and called me by his grace, to reveal his Son in me, that I might preach him among the Gentiles. . . . GALATIANS 1.15,16

What things were gain to me, those I have counted loss for Christ. PHILIPPIANS 3.7

WHAT difference did it make to Paul when he was converted to Christianity? 'What things were gain to me, those I have counted loss for Christ.' What things did he mean?

He meant all his religious advantages. He had had a very good start, as a young man. He felt that so far as traditions and environment and heritage and training could go, no one ever had a better start than he. That was quite true. When Paul was a young fellow, before he had ever heard of Christ, he was as likely a specimen of young manhood as you could find. He was a pure-blooded Hebrew, of the honourable clan of Benjamin—nothing foreign and doubtful about him. He had lived abroad, been born in Tarsus, but there was in him none of the laxity of the pagan world. He had been educated in Jerusalem, under the best teachers, in the school of what we might call the Puritans, or what they called the Pharisees, and he had grown up accordingly—keen, high-minded, scrupulous, earnestly religious, as those Pharisees at their best undoubtedly were. All that was on the credit side of the balance—'what things were gain to me'. And it might well seem that there was nothing on the other side. No one ever had a better start, and he seemed to have turned out the right sort of young man in every respect. His parents might indeed rejoice and be proud of him, and he might well be satisfied with his own prospects, body and soul. Anyone might have

94

been glad to be standing in his shoes. That was Paul the young man.

And he might well have continued in that even course all his life, but for two things.

(1) The first thing was that *somehow he was not satisfied*. His mind was not easy. Everybody else might be envying him, but he somehow did not feel enviable. He didn't feel as if he were really a success. For all his blamelessness, he did not feel that he had conquered evil in his own soul, or earned the love and favour of God. The people around him would not have guessed it, and perhaps at the time he hardly admitted it himself; but we can guess from some of his letters, written long afterwards, how it was with him as a young man. And so it is with many young men and women, even those who seem to have the ball at their feet. They are not happy, they are not satisfied. That was one thing about the young Paul.

(2) And the other was this. Paul heard some strange and disquieting talk about *a man called Jesus*. Where did he hear it? No doubt it was mainly from his friends the Pharisees. He was one of them. And what did they tell him? What kind of impression did they give him of this Jesus whom they had known? I want to look somewhat carefully at that question. Those Pharisees, like Paul himself, were, many of them, earnest and scrupulous men, maintaining a strict and high tradition, and determined that, however few righteous persons there might be in a city, they would be among them. They seemed to be 'wise unto salvation' if ever anybody was, and they could claim that they had earned God's favour. And now there was this Jesus, offering the love of God to everybody, making no difference, lumping them with the crowd, as if all their religious assets were no assets at all. Jesus would go and talk to all sorts of outsiders, doubtful kinds of people without much religious profession, and even godless foreigners, and talk to them as if they could claim God's

favour. And He sometimes spoke as if the righteous people, like the Pharisees, needed God's forgiveness just as much, or even more. Everybody needed God's forgiveness, and nobody could do anything to earn His love. They must all take their place together as God's unworthy children. But all that was profoundly shocking to the Pharisees. It seemed to wipe out moral distinctions, lumping the good and the bad together, and imperilling the interests of true religion. So they opposed Jesus with all their power, and eventually joined with those others who were taking steps to get Jesus put out of the way; and so He was condemned and crucified.

That was what Paul heard from his brother Pharisees. And of course this Jesus seemed to him a dangerous person, and he joined the anti-Christian movement and became a leader in it. Jesus' teaching was all just the opposite of what he had been brought up on. To listen to that sort of thing would be treason to all his traditions; it would mean to throw overboard all that he had built his life on. How could he ever dream of doing such a thing as that? How could he?

But that was just what Paul did. 'What things were gain to me, those I counted loss for Christ.' That is what happened in his conversion. In the verse from Galatians he says: 'When it pleased God to reveal his Son to me.' He came to see that Christ was not an impostor, but the Son of God, and then he saw everything with new eyes.

I want to mention three ways in which that made a difference to Paul.

(1) *It saved Paul from himself.* Hitherto, even in his religious zeal, he had been concentrating on himself; trying to save his own soul; cultivating his own character; watching, as it were, his own step; trying to win God's favour for himself by his own goodness, his own righteousness. And even when he was most earnest about it, the whole business was very self-centred. And so it was not successful. For self-centred-

ness is the very thing from which we need to be delivered. That is what is wrong with us. Each one of us makes himself the centre of his universe; that is to say, puts himself where God ought to be. That is what is wrong and needs to be put right. And how could we possibly put that right by concentrating on ourselves, on saving ourselves? We cannot save ourselves from ourselves, and when we try we make things worse than ever, because again we are concentrating on ourselves.

But how common that mistake still is, just among earnest people! Earnest people who have never really understood the Gospel. What Paul learned in becoming a Christian was that he could not save himself. He could never possibly *earn* the love and favour of God, and to try merely makes one self-righteous. But he didn't need to earn God's love. God loved him already, just as he was, and had shown it in Christ. 'God commendeth his own love toward us, in that, while we were yet sinners, Christ died for us.' That is what Paul discovered. And so now he need not worry about himself any more. He can be God-centred. That is how Christ saved Paul from himself. And that is the very meaning of salvation.

(2) *God gave Paul something to do in the world.* And of course that was part of the process of saving him from himself. Look again at this verse in Galatians: 'When it pleased God, who set me apart from my mother's womb and called me by his grace, to reveal his Son to me, that I might preach him among the nations. . . .' That verse contains a whole doctrine of election. But what a wholesome conception of election, and how different from what people often imagine! Election means God choosing people, but not just choosing them for their own salvation, as His special favourites, but rather choosing them to do something, and usually something difficult and costly. Certainly that was true of the

'chosen people', as we call them, the Hebrew nation. God chose them, not to have a good time, but to spread the knowledge of Him among other nations, at the cost of great suffering. And Paul says that God had chosen him before he was born and then in due time revealed Christ to him, that he might 'preach him among the nations'. I don't need to tell you what it cost Paul in persecutions and hardships. He was a hunted homeless man for the rest of his life. But it was worth it all. For God had saved Paul from himself and given him something to do in the world.

Isn't that always part of what is meant by salvation? And don't you young men and women know in your hearts that nothing better could happen to you than this: that God should save you from yourselves not only by assuring you of His love, but by giving you something to do? It is only to a very small minority that God gives the task He gave Paul—of preaching the Gospel. But nothing is more important in the world today than that Christian laymen and women should regard their various professions and occupations as vocations to which God has called them, in which they can live as Christian laymen in secular life. My friends, young men and women, may God, who chose you before you were born, and calls you by His grace, give you each one something to do.

(3) In becoming a Christian, *Paul discovered the unity of all mankind in Christ*, and this is closely connected with what I have said already about his conversion. All these things went together. He had to carry the Gospel to the outsiders, to the nations, because all his proud Jewish exclusiveness had been broken down by Christ. All his ancestral advantages had to be thrown overboard, and to be counted a dead loss, because Christ is for everybody and all the differences are insignificant: in Christ Jesus there is neither Jew nor Greek, barbarian nor Scythian, slave nor free man. All are one in

Christ. That was a tremendous innovation in Paul's thinking, and it came to him with his conversion.

There are various ways in which this could be applied most relevantly to the problems of our time. For example, to the question of racial discrimination. In the light of Christ, all races are the same. When you get down to the deepest level, there is no difference between one race and another, because all are sinners and the grace of God extends to all alike. In many ways we still need to learn that lesson.

But there is another application that I want to make especially. I want to remind you of the unity in Christ of all the churches. Of course Paul did not make that application, because the Church was not divided into denominations in his time. But he would surely have approved of our making this application. Only, he would have been quite astounded at there being any need of it. Paul would have been profoundly shocked at the very idea that the Church should be divided into separate churches, denominations competing with each other in any one place. He was once profoundly shocked when he heard that among the Christians at Corinth there was a suggestion of separate parties—a Paul-party, an Apollos-party, a Peter-party, and a Christ-party. He asked, with strong indignation: Was Paul crucified for you? Or were you baptized in the name of Paul?

You and I know of the historical causes that have divided the Church in the modern world into separate communions, and many of us naturally prize our own ancestral traditions, just as Paul prized his. But so far as our traditions are separating us from each other, surely we ought to be able to see that Christ is greater than all of them, and that He may be calling us to sacrifice even things that are familiar and dear to us if they are hindering that enrichment which Christ can give us in unity with each other. 'What things were gain to me, those I counted loss for Christ.' Isn't God leading us on towards the point when we shall say that, and say it gladly, about some of the things that separate us as Churches from each other?

Certainly in recent years God has shown the separated Churches in a new way that they are one in Christ. He has given Christians a new unity with each other. And if we are Christians we must work and pray for the hastening of the time when that unity will be more visible, and therefore richer and more effective; that the prayer of our Great High Priest may be fulfilled in His followers: 'that they all may be one; as Thou, Father, art in me, and I in Thee, that they also may be in us; that the world may believe that Thou hast sent me.'

And unto Him be glory, both now and for ever. AMEN.

12. ALL SAINTS AND ALL SINNERS

*And he turned to the woman, and said unto Simon, Seest thou this
woman?* LUKE 7.44

TODAY is the Festival of All Saints, and you may wonder
what connection my text has with it. But I hope you will
see before I have finished.

The Catholic tradition has its Calendar of Saints, but the
Churches of the Reformation have never made so much of
that. Indeed it is sometimes maintained that Protestantism
recognizes no saints in that special sense; not because it does
not honour sanctity, but rather because it has rediscovered
what sainthood meant in the New Testament. Who are 'the
saints' in the New Testament? They are not a spiritual elite
—that is not how the word is used. The saints were the
whole body of Christians; all Christ's people are 'called to be
saints'. But that did not mean that all Christians are regarded
as having reached a sinless perfection. In that sense there are
no saints in the New Testament, for even the best of Christians on earth are far from perfect. The only saints in the
New Testament are forgiven sinners, always ready to ack-
nowledge that they are utterly dependent on the mercy and
grace of God.

And now let us look at this story from St. Luke's Gospel.
There are three main figures in this domestic scene:
Simon the Pharisee, who was host; Jesus the rabbi, who was
guest; and the fallen woman, who was uninvited. It was her
presence that started the conversation. Jesus says to the
Pharisee: 'Do you see this woman?' But what strikes me as
I read the words is that Jesus and His host were not really
seeing the same woman, because they were looking at her

with such different eyes. The Pharisee saw nothing but her shame, her disreputableness, the mess she had made of her life. But Jesus saw something more: He saw the woman whom God had created, the woman that God had intended her to be, yes, and even the woman that by God's grace she might yet become. They were seeing different things as they looked: Simon the Pharisee and Jesus the Friend of Sinners. And the question that Jesus put to him comes to us also, and asks us with what kind of eyes we look upon our fellow-creatures. What do we see when we look at someone who seems to have made a mess of his life?

(1) Sometimes we just see the wretched fellow *as he is*, in all his shame and failure, and our hearts reject him, without imagination or pity. You meet a drunken man staggering home on a Saturday night, with a mouth as foul as his hands; or you encounter an unkempt unshaven tramp who accosts you with the unmistakable whining voice; or perhaps you rub shoulders with a fellow-student who has done something disreputable. And you look at the man (or woman) with a cold virtuous disapproval, a kind of protective self-righteousness which makes a safe hedge between you and him. He is undeserving, he has made his bed and must lie on it. And as you look at him, there is something complacent and merciless in your attitude. Isn't there? Aren't we all sometimes like that?

If so, then we can understand how that Pharisee felt. He was so like us—especially like those of us who take our religion seriously. He was very much in earnest. He was sure that he was right. It was, as it were, across a gulf that he looked at this woman. She was disreputable, she was known in the town to be a fallen woman. St. Luke makes it plain in the telling of the story that the Pharisee was genuinely surprised and shocked at Jesus letting the woman speak to Him or touch His feet. He thought that surely Jesus didn't know. It was not the only time a Pharisee was shocked at Jesus. They couldn't understand His interest in such disreputable outsiders. And it was just because they were so earnest and righteous that they were so surprised. That is exactly how it was with this Pharisee in the story. He had a neat and tidy mind. In his mind all humanity were divided into two classes, the good people (of whom he was one) and the bad people. He had no use at all for the bad people, no interest in them. That woman was one of the bad people. And that was an end of it. He looked at the woman, and he said to himself, 'She is a sinner' and he had nothing more to say.

And so often you and I are like that. There is so much of the Pharisee in most of us who call ourselves Christians; and we look across a gulf at the sinner and dismiss him as a sinner. That is all we see.

(2) But sometimes, if our hearts are at all pitiful or imaginative, we see, for a moment, something more. We see the sinner *as he or she might have been*. And that is more like the spirit of Jesus.

We know enough about Jesus to assure us that when He looked upon that woman, or any woman like her, He saw her as one who had been created to be a daughter of God. Perhaps His imagination travelled back through the years to a pure happy Galilean home, and in it a cradle, and in the cradle a child—the child that this woman had once been, an innocent babe, a gift of God to this world. And then perhaps in His fancy He saw children playing in the street of a Galilean village, and among them the girl that this woman had been, playing happily among her companions, with the simplicity of nature which Jesus seems to have found, and delighted to find, in children. That was what the woman had been. If only her girlhood had been soundly guided and moulded in the love of what is good, how differently things might have turned out! But somebody led her astray (and Jesus would say: Woe be to that person!). And so the girl grew up into this ruined and disreputable woman, the girl who might have grown into a good happy wife and mother, whose children would rise up and call her blessed. That was what might have been. And it would be so like Jesus to think of that.

Another case was the case of Zacchaeus, the wretched little skinflint and cheat of a tax-collector, to whom everybody gave the cold-shoulder. Jesus said, 'That man also is a son of Abraham.' He was once the boy of some mother in Israel who hoped great things for him, and if only he had been in the hands of the right people, he might have become a true son of God. That was how Jesus saw people.

If we had more of His spirit, we would look on life's failures with more imagination, more compassion. And perhaps instead of building a protective wall between ourselves and the sinner, we would begin to tell ourselves that there isn't so very much difference between us. We might have been worse than he, if we had grown up in his surroundings; and if he had had our opportunities, he might have been a better man than we have ever been. Perhaps he even is!

You remember what has so often been told of Bradford, the English preacher-martyr of the sixteenth century. Once when he was preaching in the open air, a condemned criminal was led past him on his way to the gallows. Bradford stopped in his preaching and pointed and said: 'There, but for the grace of God, goes John Bradford.' And here is a companion story about the great Edinburgh preacher Dr Alexander Whyte. One week a very well-known and highly respected Edinburgh citizen was suddenly arrested for embezzlement and sent to prison. The following Sunday morning Dr Whyte was in his vestry when the church bells began to ring. He turned to his colleague and said: 'Do you hear those Sabbath bells? He hears them in his prison cell this morning. Man, it might have been me.'

When you look on one of life's tragic failures, do you ever tell yourself humbly that, but for the grace of God, it might have been you? And do you ever think also, with compassion, of what that sinner might have been, by God's grace—as I am sure Jesus did when He said 'Seest thou this woman?'

(3) But, there is yet another thing Jesus saw when He looked on this woman, and this is by far the most important of all. He saw *what she could still become*, by the grace of God.

In the whole story of the ministry of Jesus, is there anything more extraordinary than the way in which He went to the most unlikely-looking people, people who had made a mess of their lives, and spoke to them with a kind of supernatural hopefulness, about what they could yet become? He thought not just of what they had once been in the innocence of childhood, and what they might have been if they had not gone wrong. How falsely sentimental that can become, that dwelling on the pathos of the 'might-have-been', if there is nothing more. But with Jesus there was more. He looked at those people with the indefatigable faith that they could yet be made into sons and daughters of God.

He looked at Zacchaeus, whom everybody despised, and He made up His mind that it could be done. So He stopped on the road, and called to Zacchaeus to come down from the tree and take Him to his house. And salvation came to the man's house that day. How often Jesus did that kind of thing! He would say to an unpromising sinner: 'Your sins are forgiven: go and sin no more.' To the astonishment of the Pharisee, He says to this woman: 'Your sins are forgiven, your faith has saved you; go in peace.' And do you see how at the end of the story the Pharisee and the sinful woman seem to have changed place with each other unawares? The

Pharisee is righteous and content, but it is not he that has the makings of sainthood. Jesus is far more hopeful about the woman, because into her life there have come the great realities of repentance and forgiveness, and that is the only way to sainthood, the only kind of sainthood there is in the Church of Christ.

That kind of thing is all over the Gospel story. And one extraordinary result of this is that throughout the rest of the New Testament the word 'sinner' is used in a different way altogether. The sinners now are not a class apart, a bunch of disreputable outsiders. 'Sinner' now means everybody, at least every Christian, every true member of the Christian Church, because that is what this new community is. The Church of Christ is not a society of righteous people who have a good right to be there, but a community of forgiven sinners. Some of them were once Pharisees (as was the great Apostle Paul himself). But they wouldn't be in the Church of Christ if they were depending on that. These are the Pharisees who came to call themselves sinners and to take their place with all other sinners at God's mercy-seat, depending on the divine forgiveness. And these are the saints of the New Testament. Calvin points out beautifully in one place how in the Creed the communion of saints is followed immediately by the forgiveness of sins. 'I believe in the holy Catholic Church, the communion of saints, the forgiveness of sins.'

And now at length we are no longer talking of other people, whether saints or sinners. Now we are talking of ourselves. You and I, my friends, are called to be saints in that sense—called into a life in which we every day confess our sins, and receive forgiveness, and accept the grace of a new beginning, and so, as the days go by, become more like the men and women God meant us to be.

So the Festival of All Saints becomes the festival of all

sinners—all sinners who are willing to cast themselves on the grace and mercy of God. And He will 'make them to be numbered with His saints in glory everlasting'.

13. THESE ARE WRITTEN THAT YE MIGHT BELIEVE

And many other signs truly did Jesus in the presence of his disciples, which are not written in this book. But these are written that ye might believe that Jesus is the Christ, the Son of God, and that believing ye might have life in his name. JOHN 20.30, 31

THESE words, coming almost at the end of the Fourth Gospel, tell us why the book was written; and though they were meant to apply only to St. John's Gospel, they may very well be applied to all four Gospels, of which this is the last. Every schoolboy knows, or ought to know, that the Gospels are four parallel accounts of the life of Jesus. They do the same thing four times over: sometimes in very different words, but sometimes in almost the same words, because the one borrowed from the other. And these four little books between them occupy a large part—not as much as half, but much more than a third, of the whole bulk of the New Testament.

(1) *Why were they written?* The first and most obvious answer is that they were written because people wanted a biography of Jesus, or at least a sketch of His life, such as in modern Britain would be required for the *Dictionary of National Biography*. And that answer has a good deal of truth in it. But not anything like the whole truth. These four books that we call the Gospels can hardly be called even sketch biographies of Jesus, they are so selective. It goes without saying that, as our text has it, Jesus did many things that are not written in St. John's Gospel; and in the next chapter, at the very end, the writer says, with a touch of oriental hyperbole, that if all the things Jesus did were written

down they would fill more books than the whole world could contain. And the reason why these biographies of Jesus were so selective was because they were written for a definite practical purpose. They were not meant for a dictionary of biography, they were not intended for the reference department of a public library; they were written because they were required by the Church for the work of spreading and handing down the Christian faith. They were written because the Church could not convey its distinctive message without telling the story of the life of Jesus.

Doubtless a certain element of legend crept into the telling of the story, and also perhaps a certain element of mysterious allegory mixed with historical fact. That is especially true of this Gospel of St. John, which came to be known as 'the spiritual Gospel'. And yet this writer whom we call John is more concerned than any other writer in the New Testament to insist that we are here dealing, not with a sublime phantasy, but with the story of a human life lived in the flesh on the soil of Palestine. That is why the four Gospels were written: because without the telling of that story the meaning of Christianity cannot be expressed at all.

Now that is something immensely important. The Christain message is fundamentally a story. It cannot be reduced to a system of general timeless truths, a kind of concentrated essence which can be squeezed out and left while the pulp of historical fact is left behind. Christianity is not simply an ethic or a philosophy. As it has sometimes been put, the Christian message is not an imperative, but an indicative; and not a present or a timeless indicative, but a past indicative, the telling of an old old story, about an actual life lived in a particular country at a particular time, the life of a man called Jesus, who 'suffered under Pontius Pilate'.

The story is not always easy to understand. It has its own problems. But how thankful we ought to be that, amid all our doubts and perplexities, our sometimes bewildered seeking after truth, we have something as definite as that on which to begin, and to which we can continually go back—the story of Jesus.

(2) But our text goes on to say much more than that about why the Gospels were written. 'These things are written *that ye may believe that Jesus is the Christ, the Son of God.*' That implies that this is not merely a biography. It is a story with a plot. And it is a superhuman plot, a divine plot. Christianity is not merely a story about Jesus. It is a story about God, about the works of God, about the purpose of God.

What is meant by believing that Jesus is the Christ, the Messiah? What does that ancient Hebrew term mean to us in the modern world? Does it mean anything vital? Yes, indeed. It immediately takes us away back to that remarkable conviction which you find running right through the Old Testament, long long before the time of Jesus, that God had a purpose for His people, that God was working in history, and that He would in the end establish His kingdom of peace and righteousness. Doubtless the people of Israel often under-stood that in a narrow nationalistic way, as if they were the chosen people of God in a selfishly superior sense. But they came to learn something better and wider too. And when Christianity came, then the chosen people was transformed into a universal community, based not on race or blood, but on faith in God through Jesus Christ, a people called out of every tribe and tongue and people and nation, to be the nucleus of a new and redeemed mankind with Christ as its King in God's universal Kingdom. The word 'Messiah', 'Christ', carries all that with it. The story that Christianity tells is as long as that, running right through human history.

Yes, but it is much longer than that. Our text says: 'that ye may believe that Jesus is the Christ, the Son of God.' And

St. John means that in a sense that lifts the story beyond the realm of history altogether, for both its beginning and its ending. It stretches away far beyond terrestrial history, both ways. It is not merely a story of a human life on earth, or even of the whole of human history on earth. It is now a story that begins in heaven and ends in heaven. It begins away back at the dawn of time, telling of how God created all things by His Word, and created man in His image, and then of how man fell away from God—mysteries which cannot be described in plain historical terms at all, but only in the highly pictorial terms of Christian mythology. And as for the end of the story, that again lies in the mysterious future, beyond the end of history, and can only be told with the kind of imagery that we find in the Book of Revelation. It is a story that runs from eternity to eternity, and tells of the working out of God's redemptive purpose, His plot. And that is the story in the very centre of which we set Jesus when we say we believe that He is the Christ, the Son of God. For the story which begins in Heaven comes down to earth, and runs through terrestrial history, and through your life and mine, whether we will or no. And the central chapter, which is the clue to the whole plot, is firmly laid upon the soil of earth in the land of Palestine: it tells of how the Word of God, through whom He made the worlds, became flesh, of how the Son of God became man, for man's redemption, in Jesus Christ.

Now, if that story is true, it sheds a new light on everything else in the world. That story, running from eternity to eternity, and dipping down into history, gives a new meaning to the whole of history. It is very remarkable how many books are being written in our time on the question whether human history has any meaning, any pattern, any direction. To a great many people in the ancient world history had no meaning, because their minds were dominated by what is called the cyclic view of history, the idea that history is a process which repeats itself in never-ending cycles, without any permanent advance or any goal or purpose. It leads nowhere. And to a great many people in the modern world that nightmare has come back in an even more dreadful form. They had an easy optimistic dream of human progress towards a Utopia, but that has been shattered by the events of our age, and they have nothing to take its place. So amid the utter confusion and horror of these times, human history seems to them like 'a tale told by an idiot, full of sound and fury, signifying nothing'. That is what has awakened the question: Has history any meaning? And that is how Christianity has rediscovered that it has an answer, that it has a momentous interpretation of the meaning of history in its story of the incarnation of the Son of God, as the Messiah of God's redeeming purpose for the world.

And even if that is a subject of deep and difficult discussion among philosophers and theologians today, it is also something that every one of us can get hold of when our minds are staggered by the confusion and tragedy of the world. We can come back to the tale told by Christianity about what God has done and is doing with mankind through Jesus Christ our Lord.

(3) But our text says even something more, even something without which it would lose its point: something which makes the story to be not merely a biography, not merely a clue to the meaning of history, but *a Gospel*. 'These things are written that ye might believe that Jesus is the Christ, the Son of God, and that believing ye might have life through His name.' The story was to bring to men not merely a new belief, but with it a new life. That is why these four books were called Gospels, the Gospel according to Matthew, Mark, Luke and John. 'Gospel' means good news.

When the apostles went out into the world, there were

plenty of men everywhere who were badly in need of something, whether they were quite conscious of it or not. They were in confusion, and sometimes in despair, not just about history, but about themselves. They were in the grip of evil ways and customs, in the grip of care and fear and chaos. They had no inward freedom, and they did not know how to make a new beginning, even if they ever admitted to themselves that they wanted to do it. And the apostles went and told them the story of Jesus Christ, of His incarnation, of His life and words and works, of His death and resurrection and ascension and the coming of the Holy Spirit; told it not as the biography of Jesus, but as the story of God Himself bearing the sins of men and offering them forgiveness and a new beginning and the life which is life eternal. And that story brought men to repentance and reconciliation, to God and to each other; it brought release and pardon and the beginning of a new kind of life, in which men, being delivered from themselves, found themselves again in the service of God and of their fellow men. And it is to that end that the story is still told from every Christian pulpit. There are still plenty of people everywhere who need something, they know not what. They need release, they need a new beginning. We all need it, over and over again, every day of our lives. And the Christian Gospel offers it to us. The Christian story, when we hear it with our ears and with our hearts, brings us to repentance and gives us liberation. It leads us into a way of life in which we confess our sins every day and receive forgiveness and a new beginning, and so come to 'die unto sin and live unto God through Jesus Christ our Lord'.

'These things are written—that you might have life through His name.'

Eternal Father, without whose blessing all gain is loss, and all labour is vain, we beseech Thee to follow with Thy blessing our meditation this day on Thy truth, that we may know the truth and the truth may make us free. Through Jesus Christ our Lord.

II
A SERIES OF SERMONS
FOR LENT AND EASTERTIDE

14. SIN AND FORGIVENESS

If we say that we have no sin, we deceive ourselves, and the truth is not in us. If we confess our sins, he is faithful and righteous to forgive us our sins, and to cleanse us from all unrighteousness.   1 JOHN 1.8, 9

A century and a half ago a great German philosopher said: 'I have no time for penitence.' Half a century ago a distinguished British scientist said: 'The higher man of today is not troubling about his sins.' And much more recently an American social psychologist spoke of the sense of sin as 'a psychopathic aspect of adolescent mentality'. There you have a crescendo of sentiments, all in one strain, running through a hundred and fifty years of the modern world, and it seems to suggest that the whole of the traditional Christian teaching about sin and repentance and forgiveness has been becoming more and more unacceptable and unintelligible to the modern mind. Moreover, the 'modern mind' means not simply our contemporaries, but ourselves, Christians as well as non-Christians. And therefore it is very likely that those sentiments which I have quoted awaken a sympathetic echo in many of our minds—an echo which conflicts with the sound of the familiar words of my text about sin and forgiveness.

I would like to try to put into words what many a man or woman of today half unconsciously thinks on this matter. It might be something like this. 'When I have done something unworthy, when I have fallen short of the ideal in my conduct, the only wholesome course is to forget about it as quickly as possible and leave it behind without repining. When our pious forefathers groaned over their sins and were greatly concerned about obtaining God's forgiveness, it was because they were afraid of the punishment God would inflict, perhaps the pains of hell fire. But that was an unworthy obsession, for it is not the punishment that really matters, but the wrong-doing in itself; and once it has been done, it cannot be undone by any amount of penitence. What is past is past, and no one, not even God, can change it now. No one can atone for my wrong-doing except myself, and I can only atone for it by leaving it behind, making any possible reparation to any one I have injured, and then going on to better things. Therefore I will not waste time "crying over spilt milk". I will not brood over past failure. I will not cultivate a sense of sin. I am not concerned about forgiveness for the past, but about doing better in the future. I have no time for penitence.'

Isn't that what many a modern man is inclined to think? And doesn't it sound wholesome to our modern minds? Doesn't it contain a good deal of truth?

But is it the whole truth? I would like to try to show that it leaves out a vast amount of reality, and that if it poses as the whole truth, it becomes tremendously naïve, and betrays a profound ignorance of human nature, and even of modern psychology. Let us think.

Isn't there something extraordinarily naïve and unrealistic about this talk of gaily forgetting our moral failures and going on our way rejoicing, to do better next time? How can we do that if we really care about right and wrong, good and bad? How can we be complacent about our misdeeds, if we really believe that these things are the most important things in the world? I am not saying, for the moment, that we ought to brood and worry over our failures, but simply that we shall inevitably feel like that about them, with shame and pain, if we have any higher life at all. It may not help us, it may even hinder and weaken us; but these considerations in themselves will not prevent our brooding and worrying, if we really care about these great issues of good and evil. If we can do wrong, and go on our way gaily without a pang, that simply means that we do not greatly care—that, as people say nowadays, we 'couldn't care less'. But then, of course, we shall not go on to better things, but to the same old things over again, the same sins repeated for ever, world without end. If we do care, if we have any seriousness and sincerity, we cannot treat our sins just like that. It can't be as easy as that. No decent man can treat his sins in just that easy way.

But what then? Are we to conclude after all that every serious modern man has a deep sense of sin? No, indeed. I don't believe he has. But I believe that very often he has a much less wholesome substitute, and that is what the psycho-pathologists get hold of. I will try to explain. The typical modern man does not understand theological jargon, and the very phrase 'a sense of sin' may be a mystery to him. But there is another kind of jargon with which he is very much at home, and which may help out my argument—the jargon of modern psychology. Every schoolboy knows what is meant by 'the inferiority complex'. Now it seems to me that a great many serious-minded people today are suffering from what I may call a moral-inferiority complex, or perhaps a 'moral-failure' complex. They have an uneasy sense of something being wrong with their lives. They do not confess their sins to God or man, not even to themselves. They do not consciously accuse themselves, for they have a protective pride which is part of the whole situation. Their companions might never guess that they were not satisfied with themselves, but might think rather the reverse; for, as the psychologists tell us, the inferiority complex easily passes over into the superiority complex, which is but the other side of the same unwholesome state of mind. And it is all sub-conscious. It is a kind of 'skeleton in the cupboard' which a man can't face because he doesn't know what to do with it. But though it is repressed it festers uneasily beneath the surface, with the effect of paralysing moral endeavour, inhibiting any new beginnings. It is not what Christians call a 'sense of sin', but something far less wholesome, a kind of secular substitute. Perhaps this is the pathological 'guilt complex' which psychologists treat as a malady. And it could become a malady. So it is not the genuine sense of sin that is 'psychopathic', but this secular substitute, which develops in an age of unbelief under the surface of a secular complacency: the 'moral-failure complex'.

Now modern psychology, which has taught us so much about the pathology of repressed complexes, has also told us how they may be cured. The cure is to get the complex dragged up into the light of day. Very often it turns out to have had a quite trivial origin, perhaps some psychological shock received in childhood and long forgotten. As soon as it is discovered and consciously faced, it loses its terrors, which had no real foundation, and the mind is healed. But can that apply to what I have called the moral-failure complex? Surely not. For in this case the root-cause is not trivial, the trouble has a real foundation which the man is not facing; namely, the fact that he has been living unworthily, he is a moral failure, his life has been wrong, he has given way to evil. That is a hard fact, and the sting is not removed from it when it is brought into the light of day. That is why people unconsciously repress it, refuse to face it. So the technique of psycho-analysis taken by itself cannot meet the situation and cure the sick soul. What then is the solution of this problem?

There is no solution on the merely secular level, the level of what is sometimes called 'mere morality'. That is where we see the bankruptcy of the attempt to have morality without religion, to have goodness without God. A secular morality, without any God, has no way of dealing with its failures, because the moralist can never forgive himself.

But the situation is quite other when you bring in— GOD. Then the consciousness of moral failure becomes something different. It becomes a sense of sin against God, a sense of having betrayed the love of God. Then it is no longer merely a matter of dragging up our repressions into the light of day, but rather into the light of God. As the Psalmist put it: 'Thou hast set our iniquities before thee, our secret sins in the light of thy countenance.'

But doesn't that seem to make the situation worse than ever? Yes, worse than ever. But it also makes it better than ever, with a quite new possibility, because of the divine forgiveness. We cannot forgive ourselves, and the moral law cannot forgive us. But God can forgive us—God, who is the very source and ground and end of our existence. 'If we confess our sins, he is faithful and righteous to forgive us our sins, and to cleanse us from all unrighteousness.' So we can accept His forgiveness, and find release and a new beginning.

Isn't that what we see happening time after time in the story of the ministry of Jesus? Isn't that what He was continually doing to people? He would go and talk to a sinner who was unhappy, but didn't know what was wrong with himself, or couldn't face it. And Jesus would say: 'Your sins are forgiven, go in peace and sin no more.' And the man made a new start. Of course he did sin again, time after time, as we all do every day. But now he had the secret of new beginnings.

Is that unwholesome? Is that morbid? That consciousness of sin against God, and the reality of the divine forgiveness? Nay, it is the one secret of healthy living. What is morbid is the secular substitute, the false guilt-complex which never gets any further because there is no faith in God.

Why is it that such maladies as neurasthenia, nervous break-down, are so common in our modern world? Is it entirely unconnected with the fact that there are now so many serious-minded people who have no belief in God and therefore have no secret for dealing with their moral failures? They cannot lightly shake off the memory of them, because they take life seriously. Yet they cannot face the memory, because they know nothing of divine forgiveness. And so their consciousness of failure, instead of becoming a wholesome sense of sin, which can lead to forgiveness and release, is repressed until it becomes a morbid complex, with paralysing effects. Their sorrow is what St. Paul so vividly calls 'the sorrow of the world, which worketh death'. It needs to be turned into what he calls the 'godly sorrow', which 'worketh repentance unto salvation, and bringeth no regret', because it leads to forgiveness.

Now that gives you what is part of the very pattern of the Christian life. And thus in the true life of a Christian there is no room for the morbid guilt-complex, with its paralysing effect. It no longer gets its chance to develop. Not because the man never sins, has left sin entirely behind. No, indeed. And not because he is never troubled about his sins; not because he has no sense of sin. But because he is continually, every day, using the liberating secret, humbly confessing his sins, accepting forgiveness and the grace of a new beginning, and so, as life goes on, more and more 'dying to sin' and 'living to God'. That is the health of the human soul.

Today I have not even touched on the question of how all this is connected with the Cross of Christ. That is what I hope to come to in the next two sermons. Today I have tried to prepare the way for that by showing that when Christians speak of the sense of sin and the divine forgiveness, they are speaking of real things which are vitally connected with the health of the soul. That is good modern psychology.

But it is not modern psychology that I am preaching. It is ancient Christianity, in its very essence. In the words of our text: 'If we say that we have no sin, we are deceiving ourselves, and the truth is not in us.' That is, we are making an escape. We are running away from reality. But the text goes on: 'If we confess our sins, God is faithful and righteous to forgive us our sins, and to cleanse us from all unrighteousness.' That is the wholesome realism of Christian faith.

15. WHY DID JESUS DIE?

My subject, in this Passion Sunday sermon, is: Why did Jesus die? That sounds a simple question, but it is really a complex one—several questions in one. It may mean several different things. It may mean: What were the motives that led the Jewish religious authorities to wish to get Jesus put out of the way? Or it may mean: Why did Jesus Himself choose the path of the Cross? What was in His mind? But it may mean yet another question—a more mysterious one which goes beyond the historical realm altogether, goes right up into the realm of Divine Providence: What is the ultimate meaning of the crucifixion of Jesus in the eternal counsel and purpose of God?

I want to take up these three questions in turn, leading on from the simplest to the deepest.

(1) *Why did they get Him put to death?* What made the Jewish religious leaders do such a terrible thing? They were not wicked and godless men. The Pharisees, who were the first to turn against Him, were very earnest men, very religious and circumspect and devoted. Why did they turn against Jesus? Undoubtedly it was because they regarded Him as a dangerous teacher, a heretical rabbi, a false prophet. They were very orthodox and conventional; but this new rabbi from Nazareth, who had never been properly trained, was unorthodox, unconventional, outspoken, not very careful about their ancestral religious traditions, not a very strict Sabbatarian, as they understood it, and not very particular about the company He kept.

And there I believe we come to what is most significant of all for our present purpose. The very first thing that turned the religious leaders against Jesus and shocked them more than anything else was this: His attitude towards sinners, His way of mixing with sinners. I mean the people of openly sinful and godless life, disreputable people, outsiders, all those men and women who in the Gospels are lumped together in that familiar phrase, 'publicans and sinners'. These people were beyond the pale of religion, and no self-respecting rabbi would be seen talking to them. But Jesus seemed to be more interested in these people than He was in anybody else: and He practically said that God was too.

So Jesus would accept invitations to the houses of wealthy sinners, and He would go and talk with disreputable sinners. He got the doubtful reputation of being 'a friend of publicans and sinners'. Nothing in the accounts of Jesus in the Gospels is more unmistakable than that. It became a matter of common gossip. The Scribes and Pharisees used to say to each other, with a good deal of self-righteous head-shaking: 'This man receives sinners and eats with them.' And Jesus said to those Pharisees: 'The publicans and the prostitutes go into God's Kingdom before you.' He meant, of course, that they were all sinners together, there were no righteous people, they all needed God's forgiveness. Only, He was more hopeful about the outsiders, because they were more ready to admit it.

Now all that was genuinely shocking to the religious leaders, the Scribes and Pharisees. Jesus seemed to be subverting all moral distinctions, lumping together the good and the bad, saying to notorious sinners: 'Your sins are forgiven.' And that was the very first thing that turned the leaders against Him—those leaders who ultimately brought about His death. So that is the answer to our first question.

That is why they plotted against His life: because He was a friend of sinners.

(2) *Why did Jesus Himself choose to die?* Why did He choose the path of the Cross? But did He choose the Cross? We must be very careful about that, because that has sometimes been said in quite false and artificial ways. One imaginative modern writer has pictured the matter as if Jesus deliberately planned to get Himself crucified, as a kind of challenge to His nation, and has even suggested that Jesus compounded with Judas to have Himself betrayed. That is surely an artificial idea. But apart from such modern speculations, people have often thought of Jesus as setting out on life with the perfectly clear knowledge of a divine plan of salvation by which He was to die on a cross to make atonement for the sins of the world; so that from the start He accepted the Cross as a thing that was 'according to plan'. Surely that is too simple. That does not do justice to what Jesus did and suffered. That makes it far easier than it really was. That would diminish the glory of the Passion, because it would mean that Jesus was playing a pre-arranged part in a drama in which everything was clear from the start, the plot and the suffering and the triumphant conclusion. Nay, but the ordeal He had to face was much harder than that. He had to go forward in the dark, walking by faith, and not by sight.

And what darkness it became, when it began to be clear that His own people were turning against Him and plotting His death! That must have seemed a very dreadful prospect, a thing almost too dreadful to be true, not just because it meant for Him a criminal's shameful death, but because it seemed to mean a complete failure and collapse of all He had ever lived for, as if God Himself had given Him up. That was not a climax according to plan. Nay, rather, we know from the Gospels that when Jesus saw it coming He shrank

126

from it with horror (as any sane man would), and that even up to the night before His crucifixion He hoped and prayed that somehow it might not come.

Then did He not choose the path of the Cross? Yes, indeed He did. He was not a helpless victim. There was a choice before Him, and He went on with His eyes open. He *could* have saved Himself. How? By changing His course, by going in for a different kind of ministry, a more conventional kind, less embarrassing to the authorities. That is what they wanted. They were trying to frighten Him into doing it. If He had been willing to change His talk, it would have saved them a lot of trouble. And He would have saved His life.

He could have done it. And yet, of course, He couldn't do it, couldn't even for one moment begin to dream of doing it. Why not? Because it would have meant giving up His mission. And above all that would have meant giving up the sinners, giving up His shocking habit of being 'a friend of publicans and sinners'. He could not give that up. And it cost Him His life. It brought Him to crucifixion.

So, you see, whatever else we may have to say about the meaning of the death of Jesus (and I'm coming to that in a moment), it is manifestly true in the plain historical and local sense that He died for sinners, the sinners of His own immediate environment, the 'lost sheep of the house of Israel' in His own time. That was where it began—with those local sinners. It was His love for these sinners that brought Him to the Cross. And that is our second answer to the question: Why did Jesus die?

But that is not all. There is a still deeper sense in which we must ask this question.

(3) *What was the meaning of the death of Jesus in the eternal purpose of God?* There can be no doubt that the crucifixion of Jesus set people thinking more than anything else that has

127

ever happened in the history of the world. And what did they think about it? When Jesus' own followers looked back and pondered on that dreadful event, what did they make of it? In the whole history of human thought there is nothing more extraordinary than this: that the crucifixion of Jesus made people think of *the love of God*. Not simply of the love of Jesus, but of the love of God. You might have expected something very different. You might have expected these followers of Jesus to lose all faith in the love of God. In all ages good men had been asking agonized questions about the terrible things that were allowed to happen in this world. How could such things happen if there was a God in heaven who knew and cared? But now came the most dreadful thing of all—the crucifixion of Jesus, the friend of sinners. What was God doing? Where was He when Jesus died?

You remember, the ancient Greeks had a beautiful legend about Prometheus, the friend of man, who snatched fire from heaven to give light and warmth to mankind, and who suffered agonies for it under the sky of an angry God. You might have expected that the followers of the crucified Jesus would now take Him as their beloved Prometheus, and that they would altogether renounce the high God in heaven, who had let Jesus, the friend of sinners, go to His shameful death.

But that was not what happened. What happened was very different. It was this. When they thought of Jesus going to the Cross in His love for sinners, they said 'God must be like that'. Nay, but they said even more than that, something still more wonderful. Not simply 'God must be like Jesus,' but 'God was in Jesus' when He suffered and died for sinners. As St. Paul put it, 'God was in Christ, reconciling the world unto Himself'. What they saw was not: on the one hand the loving and merciful Jesus, and on the other hand the angry God. What they saw was this: on the one hand, Jesus the friend of sinners going to His death; and on the other hand, or rather (we might say) on the same hand, the God and Father of our Lord Jesus Christ, who shared Himself to the full in the sacrifice of Calvary, and who started the whole redemption process at infinite cost to Himself, because He so loved the world.

That is why Jesus died. With all the other answers that we give, we can't stop short of that deepest of all answers. Jesus died on the Cross because it was God's will to come right into our sinful fallen human situation, and, incarnate in a man, to bear upon Himself the sin of the world.

In the presence of that Cross and Passion we are all sinners. There are no righteous people. And now, on this Passion Sunday, from that Cross of Christ, God Himself is stretching out His hands to us, appealing to us to repent and return to Him and be forgiven and make a new beginning. St. Paul expressed that appeal when he said, in the words of our text: 'God commends His own love toward us in that, while we were yet sinners, Christ died for us.' And three centuries later another great saint expressed it in words of magnificent symbolism, when he said: 'It is only on a cross that a man dies with outstretched hands.'

'And now unto Him that loveth us and hath loosed us from our sins in His own blood, and hath made us kings and priests to His God and Father, to Him be glory and dominion for ever and ever.' AMEN.

16. THE ATONING SACRIFICE

God was in Christ, reconciling the world unto himself.
2 CORINTHIANS 5.19

ONE of the great discoveries of the New Testament was this: that God loves us before we have begun to be worthy of His love. He loves not only good people, but bad people. He loves us while we are yet sinners. I think that was the central thing that Paul discovered about God in becoming a Christian, and it astonished him. He had always longed to enjoy the love and favour of God, and all through his youth he had been trying hard to win it by keeping God's commandments and making himself into a good man. But he had never felt that he was succeeding in becoming a good man, and so he was not managing to earn God's love. And then suddenly, through Christ, he discovered that he didn't need to do it. God loved him already, while he was still a sinner. That was what Paul discovered; and it gave him quite a new start. Of course that discovery goes back to the story of Jesus Christ, of how He behaved towards sinners, befriended sinners; and of how He explained and defended it by teaching that God Himself is like that—as in the parable of the Prodigal Son, whose father ran out to welcome him, and the parable of the Shepherd who went out into the wilderness to find the one lost sheep. That is what Christianity discovered about God.

But now, if all that is true—if God is as willing to forgive sinners freely as the father in the parable was to forgive and welcome his prodigal son—then where is the need for anything like an atoning sacrifice? If Paul discovered that God loves us already, while we are yet sinners, how could He afterwards go on to work out elaborate doctrines of atonement through the death of Christ? To the typically modern mind nothing is more uncongenial or even unintelligible than the idea of atonement by sacrifice. And you may very well wish to ask me: What room is there for it, if God is really like the father of the Prodigal Son?

I must begin my answer by asking of you another question in return: Do you think all this costs God nothing? Is it all a kind of good-natured amnesty on God's part? Does He pass lightly over our sins, as if they did not matter much to Him? Is it all as easy as that? And if we thought of the divine forgiveness in that easy way, would it really have a liberating effect and send us forth to better things? Surely not. Surely that makes it all too cheap. The classical example of that may be found in what the German poet Heine said on his death-bed: 'God will forgive me: that is His business.' We can all see that that is a complete misunderstanding of what God's mercy means. That is what the heroic Dietrich Bonhoeffer called 'cheap grace'.

Even human mercy is not such a shallow thing as that. Suppose I have a friend who is a pure and noble soul and who loves me deeply. And suppose that I sin against his friendship behind his back, betraying him in some unworthy way, and he discovers it. What will he feel and say and do? If he were a shallow soul and our friendship were on a shallow level, he would perhaps drop me quietly altogether and ignore me ever after. Or perhaps he would gloss the matter smoothly over, and pretend that nothing had happened, so as to avoid an uncomfortable scene. But if he is indeed an honest and noble soul, and loves me deeply, he cannot take these easy ways. He will be honest and straight and agonizingly relentless—not because he does not love me, but because he does. The reconciliation will not be easy and painless; it will be costly and painful. And it is my friend, far more than I, that will pay the price and suffer the pain, because he is a better man than I, and he loves me. He will suffer grief and shame, not because of the injury done to him, but because of me. He will bear the agony of the shame of what I have done. And it is out of that whole costly experience of suffering in his heart that there will come the forgiveness, the reconciliation.

Can that be a faint analogue of the love of God which bears the sins of the world? Just because He loves us with an infinite and everlasting love, His grace cannot be 'cheap grace', His forgiveness cannot be an easy and good-natured amnesty. Just because He loves us infinitely, He suffers infinitely for our sins. And out of that suffering comes the divine atonement, the divine reconciliation. Atonement means 'at-one-ment' or reconciliation.

That brings us to the very heart and climax of our argument. For now we must face the question: What connection has that with the Cross of Christ? And why call His death an atoning sacrifice? We read in the Epistle to the Hebrews of how Christ as our High Priest offered Himself up on the Cross as a sacrifice for us. What can that mean? In the literal sense, Jesus was not a priest, but a layman. The cross on which He died was not an altar, but a gallows. His death was not a ritual sacrifice, but a judicial execution. What then do we mean by 'the atoning sacrifice'?

These very words take us right back to the Old Testament, to the preparation for Christ in ancient Israel.

Now, it is a very remarkable thing that in this matter of sin and forgiveness you find in the Old Testament two different strains which seem to contradict each other. On the one hand, you have the system of sacrifices as a divinely appointed means of having one's sins expiated and forgiven. It was not so much the flagrant transgressions of the moral law that were dealt with in that way, but rather the ceremonial offences which men might commit without any evil intent: these could be wiped out by certain sacrifices which God in His mercy had appointed. The flagrant and deliberate transgressions of the moral law were different. For these great sins men could not count on God's mercy. These things could not be expiated by the ritual sacrifices which wiped out the smaller offences.

But when you come to the great prophets, you find another strain of teaching. You find them teaching that those transgressions of the moral law were what God really cared about—injustice, cruelty, deceit, dishonesty in common life—and so long as men practised these things God took no pleasure at all in their sacrifices, and would not accept them. But also this: that if only men would repent of their evil ways and return to God, then He would freely forgive all their sins, even their most flagrant transgressions, without any distinction. Nothing was needed but genuine repentance— no sacrifices, no offerings on the altar. 'Thou desirest not sacrifice, else would I give it. Thou delightest not at all in burnt-offering. The sacrifices of God are a broken spirit: a broken and a contrite heart, O God, thou wilt not despise.' 'Let the wicked forsake his way, and the unrighteous man his thoughts; and let him return unto the Lord, and he will have mercy upon him, and to our God, for he will abundantly pardon.'

Now you might have expected that if that teaching was taken seriously, the sacrifices of the altar would be given up altogether. But that was not what happened. The sacrifices went on, and became more elaborate than ever, and even came to be applied to all kinds of sins. And so these two strains in the religion of Israel seem to go side by side, almost contradicting each other, until you come to the time of Christ and of the New Testament.

And what happened then? If the New Testament is the

fulfilment of the Old, which of these two contradictory strains did the New Testament take up and carry on to its climax and fulfilment: the strain which spoke of the need of atoning sacrifices, or that which spoke of God's absolutely free forgiveness? The breath-taking answer is: both together, and both equally, only now they have come together without any contradiction, they have both become one—because it is God Himself who both makes the sacrifice and forgives the sin. The doctrine that God freely forgives the sinner is carried further than ever in the teaching of Jesus, as in the parables of the Prodigal Son and the Lost Sheep. At the same time the long tradition of atoning sacrifice reaches its climax, but in such a way that it is completely transformed, because now it is God Himself who provides the victim, and as it were out of His own bosom, for the victim is His own Son.

What an extraordinary climax that is! Here are all the old terms of the Old Testament sacrificial system—offering, sacrifice, atonement, reconciliation, expiation. But now they receive a radically new interpretation—not only because they are applied to the death of Christ, which was not in the literal sense a sacrifice at all, but also because it is God Himself who is regarded as making the sacrifice, providing the victim, bearing the cost.

Here is the atonement, the reconciliation, which wipes out our sins; but we contribute nothing to the process, says Paul: 'it is all of God', and He 'was in Christ, reconciling the world unto Himself'. Just as Abraham did not spare his beloved son, but was ready to sacrifice him for God, so (says St. Paul), 'God did not spare His own Son, but delivered Him up (sacrificed Him) for us all'. Here is the lamb sacrificed for the sins of men; but this lamb is 'in the midst of the throne of God', this 'Lamb of God that taketh away the sin of the world' is none other than the Son of God incarnate,

God only-begotten, the Word-made-flesh. Here (according to the Epistle to the Hebrews) is the sin-offering. But now victim and Priest are one, and they are none other than the eternal Son of God, through whom He made the world, who, when He had offered Himself on the Cross, ascended into the heavens to continue His perpetual priesthood for us in the heavenly sanctuary. So the Atonement is not a sacrifice offered to God to appease His anger and to reconcile Him to us. No, it is the love of God bearing the brunt of the sin of the world that He may reconcile us to Him. That is something eternal, because God is love. It had its out-cropping into the plane of history in the Passion and Cross of Christ, and it goes on for ever more. That is the Atoning Sacrifice.

And now, finally, this question: What difference does it make?

A fortnight ago I began this series of sermons by preaching about Sin and Forgiveness. And now I want to say: What keeps the whole idea of the forgiveness of sins sound and wholesome is the Christian Gospel of the divine atoning sacrifice. If we hold that Cross of Christ before our eyes, then we shall never make the divine forgiveness either too cheap on the one hand or too impossible on the other. Some people make the one mistake, and some make the other. Some make it too cheap and easy, as if our sins did not matter much; and that is not the way to better things. Others make it too difficult, and can't forgive themselves at all, and that also is not the way to better things. But we can't make the first mistake if we remember what our sins have done to the Son of God. And we can't make the second mistake if we remember what the Son of God has done with our sins. And these two things come together in the Cross of Christ. That is the Atoning Sacrifice.

And the result is summed up in the wholesome text with

which I began this series of sermons a fortnight ago. 'If we say we have no sin, we are deceiving ourselves, and the truth is not in us. If we confess our sins, he is faithful and righteous to forgive us our sins, and to cleanse us from all unrighteousness'. (1 John 1.8, 9).

17. PALM SUNDAY

*Tell ye the daughter of Zion, Behold, thy King cometh unto thee,
meek, and sitting upon an ass, even a colt the foal of an ass.*

MATTHEW 21.5

I ONCE heard a wise man say that the best reason for learning
by heart, in one's youth, great passages of poetry is because
the poetry will then have deeper and deeper meanings put
into it by the experience of life as the years go by. When
you first learn it, you are young and immature, and it does
not mean a great deal to you. But there it is, stored up in
your mind; and as you go through life things happen, and
experience grows, and the old bit of poetry comes home to
you in new ways. You find in it something that you never
suspected, new and richer meanings that perhaps even go
beyond what the poet himself could have consciously thought
or meant. How very true that is!

And it seems to me that the same thing is true, not only
of the individual growing older through the years, but also
of the human race growing older through the centuries; and
particularly of the Church of God in the use that it makes of
what was written long ago by the poets and prophets of
Israel, as we find it in the Old Testament. I want to apply
that to the bit of poetry I have taken as our text in this Palm
Sunday service.

'Rejoice greatly, O daughter of Zion: Shout, O daughter
of Jerusalem: Behold thy King cometh unto thee: he is
righteous and victorious, he is lowly, and rides on an ass,
even on a colt the foal of an ass.' These words from Zecha-
riah 9.9 were written hundreds of years before Christianity
began, by a prophet-poet in Israel, and many a schoolboy

learned them by heart. Then one day in the lifetime of Jesus, something happened which made people think of the passage, and so it is quoted here in the New Testament. And now, after nineteen centuries, we are quoting it this morning in this Christian service. What does it mean?

Don't you see that this is one of those bits of poetic prophecy in the Old Testament which have come to mean more and more in the history of God's dealings with men, and that for us Christians, with the Gospel story behind us, it has come to mean far more than it could ever have meant for the man who first wrote it?

Let us try, then, first to see what it meant for the poet who wrote it; then what it meant for the crowd who thought of it when Jesus rode into Jerusalem; then what it meant for Jesus Himself; and then what it means to us to-day after nineteen hundred years.

(1) *What did it mean for the man who first wrote it?* He lived in the land of Israel, long before the time of Jesus. He lived in bad times, when the little country of Israel had long lost its independence, as we have seen quite a number of little countries do in our own time, when they were overwhelmed by some powerful empire. So it was with Israel. And this prophet-poet of Israel had a vision of a better time coming. He was a patriot and a liberationist, but he was also an ardent believer in God, and now he looked forward in faith to a coming day when God would again give them a king of their own. The coming king would be a liberator of their country, like so many great national liberators of whom you can think. But he would not be a warmonger. He would be a peacemaker, arriving home from his victories not on a warhorse, but on an ass, gentlest of all animals and symbol of peace. There was, no doubt, something nationalistic about this poet's dream, but it was not narrow, it was a dream of a

138

king whose peaceful kingdom would transcend all frontiers and bless all mankind; so he sang:

> Rejoice greatly, O daughter of Zion;
> Shout aloud, O daughter of Jerusalem.
> Lo, your king comes to you,
> Humble and riding on an ass,
> On a colt, the foal of an ass. . . .
> And he shall command peace to the nations.
> His dominion shall be from sea to sea,
> And from the river to the ends of the earth.

That is what it meant to the man who wrote it.

(2) *What did it mean to the people who thought of it that day, hundreds of years later, as Jesus rode into Jerusalem?* You remember the scene, how the disciples and the other pilgrims scattered green leaves and waved green branches, and sang and shouted: 'Hosanna, blessed is the kingdom that is coming, the kingdom of our ancestor David!' It does not take very much to make a crowd shout. And at that time in Israel there was popular unrest and discontent; and here was a peasant from Galilee who was going to be a people's leader. They would make him their king. It would be like the good old days of King David come back again. The people thought of the poem they had learned at school: 'Behold, thy king cometh unto thee.' Well, here he was!

Perhaps they did not know exactly what they meant. But they shouted, with warm and eager hearts. A new meaning came into the old words, from their knowledge of this beloved Galilean, Jesus. And Jesus did not despise it. He liked it much better than the stony and jealous silence of the Pharisees. The Pharisees hated this popular response, they were even shocked and wanted Jesus to stop it. But He replied: 'I tell you that if these people were to keep silent, the very stones would cry out.' It was indeed a great moment in the history of the world, as we know well. But how little they understood of what was in store—even the disciples, whose minds Jesus had been preparing, not to speak of the rest of the crowd! Their King was indeed coming into their city, but He was coming to die on a cross! How little any of them realized the depth of the situation! How little they realized what Jesus was going to have to face before the Kingdom of God could come!

We may take that crowd, with its shouting and its processing, as typifying all those people in every age who have tried to take easy and romantic views of the meaning of the Gospel. And perhaps that includes ourselves, on this Palm Sunday, though we ought to know better. Even in this chaotic age in which we live, amid all the unimaginable toil and suffering, how we still try to take easy and shallow views of how men can be saved and of how the world can be saved! We try to have a romantic version of Christianity, and we imagine that will appeal to young people and attract them: a version of the Gospel which has not much to say about heart-searching and sacrifice, not much about repentance and forgiveness and obedience and the Cross. We try to think that the Church can do its work without going very deep, and that the world can be saved by the shouting of attractive slogans from wayside pulpits. We ought to know better.

> The tumult and the shouting dies,
> The captains and the kings depart:
> Still stands Thine ancient sacrifice,
> An humble and a contrite heart.

(3) *What did it mean to Jesus?* 'Behold thy king cometh unto thee—lowly, and riding on an ass.' Jesus also was thinking that day of the little poem He had learned as a boy. What were the thoughts He had about it?

We are bound to ask that question. But we must not pretend that it is quite easy to answer. What did the whole of that triumphal procession mean to Jesus? Why did He arrange it? Or did He actually arrange it? Perhaps He did not intend it to be a triumphal procession at all. Perhaps it was the disciples and the crowd that took the matter into their own hands, as their enthusiasm broke out around Jesus. We can't be quite sure. But one thing we do know. In all that crowd, moving along the road over the shoulder of the Mount of Olives and approaching the city of Jerusalem, there was just one man with a sense of tragedy in his heart and a shadow of sorrow in his eyes, one man who was setting his teeth for a supreme ordeal, one man who, as they came in sight of the beloved city, wept over it. That was the man riding in the middle, the one whom all the crowd were joyfully hailing as their King. That was Jesus.

There, in front of them, as they came round the bend of the road, lay the towers of the city in spring sunshine; the city of David, the city of Zion, the holy city about which the Psalmists had sung so fervently, the city that had so often killed its prophets. And it was going to kill Jesus. For a long time He had seen this coming, and had tried to prepare His disciples for it. They would not believe it. They would hardly listen to His hints. But Jesus knew. And that day, amid the crowd, surely this was part of the loneliness of His Passion. The people were rejoicing, but St. Luke tells us that as they came in sight of the city, Jesus wept over it. He was not weeping for Himself, but for Jerusalem, for its blindness, for its tragedy, because it did not know the time of its visitation, and it was going to crucify its King.

> Rejoice greatly, O daughter of Zion;
> Shout, O daughter of Jerusalem.
> Behold, thy King cometh unto thee.

Yes, and their King was this Galilean peasant, going to Jerusalem to die. No one knew it except Himself. And He went on with His eyes open, and with nothing in His heart except faith towards God and love towards men. That is what it meant for Jesus.

(4) *What does it mean for us, after nineteen hundred years?*
The Cross is past, and the victory is past. When once it was
past, and people had had time to ponder on it and pass on
the story to others, then there began to arise, not just on the
slopes of the Mount of Olives, but in ever widening circles
throughout the world, the surge of joy and praise round
about Jesus: 'Unto Him that loveth us, and hath loosed us
from our sins by His own blood, and hath made us to be
kings and priests to His God and Father, to Him be glory and
dominion for ever and ever.' And now we can look back
and see what was really happening that week in Jerusalem.
This was not just the death of a prophet. This was not the
tragedy of a Galilean peasant. This was God visiting and
redeeming His people. This was God incarnate bearing upon
Himself the sin and suffering of mankind. This was God in
Christ reconciling the world to Himself. This was the beginning of a new age in the history of the world. And now,
after nineteen centuries, we can look back and see the Kingdom of Christ spreading from shore to shore, and men
coming into it from north and south, from east and west, of
every tribe and tongue and people and nation. And this
Palm Sunday we can join with the whole Church of Christ,
of every land and age, on earth and in heaven, and sing:
'Hosanna, blessed is He that cometh in the name of the Lord!'

But, my friends, let us remember that He is continually
coming to us in new and unexpected ways. Jerusalem did not
know its King when He came. And sometimes we do not
know our King when He comes to us, because He comes
with new calls and challenges, touching the affairs of our own
times; our private lives, our public lives, our use of our
money, our social relationships, our political responsibility in
these days when everyone has a vote. In all these things He
claims 'the crown rights of the Redeemer'. But when He
comes to us in these ways, it is so easy to miss His coming

altogether; to surround His name with our praises, and to be blind to the obedience that He demands in the life of a Christian citizen of the twentieth century.

That would be to repeat in our time the mistake that Jerusalem made when it rejected Him. 'He came unto His own, and His own received Him not. But to as many as did receive Him, to them He gave power to become children of God.' And He comes to us again today, to bring us to repentance, to offer us forgiveness, to call us to new obedience, to recall us to the service of His Kingdom, to set His Cross in our hearts and lives, and, amid all the challenge of life in the twentieth century, to make us kings and priests to God.

'Behold, thy King cometh unto thee.'

18. EASTER DAY

Thanks be to God, who giveth us the victory through our Lord Jesus Christ.   I CORINTHIANS 15.57

IT may be that some of you who are worshipping God this Easter morning are conscious in your minds of a certain questioning and perplexity, mingled with the joy of the Easter festival—and just because your faith means much to you and you try to understand the Bible. When you read in the Gospels the stories about the empty tomb and the appearances of the risen Christ to His disciples, you find difficulties and contradictions, and you don't know what to make of them or how to interpret them. If there are any of you who feel like that, I would like quite especially to speak to such. It is no wonder that you are sometimes mystified. It is extraordinarily difficult to say what exactly happened on the first Easter morning—to explain, as it were, the way in which God gave the victory to Jesus. I am not going to try to deal with these questions—perhaps they are unanswerable. I want rather to suggest that without having solved them we can understand and share in the faith which made these followers of Jesus in the New Testament exclaim: 'Thanks be to God, who giveth us the victory through our Lord Jesus Christ.'

The New Testament is full of the glad conviction that God had given Jesus the victory: not so much that Jesus rose from the dead as that God raised Him from the dead. Jesus had faced His ordeal, He had drunk His bitter cup, He had been obedient to the point of death, even the death of the Cross, utterly committing Himself in faith to God. And God did not fail Him, did not let Him down. God saw Him through, God brought Him through the jaws of death and raised Him up. God gave Him the victory. And through Him God gives us the victory too. So St. Peter speaks to his fellow Christians of 'God, who raised Him from the dead and gave Him glory, so that your faith and hope might be in God'. And St. Paul says, with the note of joy and praise: 'Thanks be to God, who gives us the victory, through our Lord Jesus Christ.'

But victory over what? Paul means victory over everything, over every enemy. And in this long and complicated chapter from which our text comes, which is all about resurrection, he takes a very wide sweep of the eye and gets a cosmic panorama of a victory over every possible evil, everything that has gone wrong with God's creation, all that belongs to a fallen world and a fallen human race, all the hostile powers that might be summed up as the world and sin and death. And he thanks God for giving us, through Christ, the victory over all of them.

Now, does all that bear upon the predicament of modern man here in the middle of the twentieth century? At first sight perhaps it doesn't, because Paul's language is archaic. But I believe that it does really touch the very nerve of modern man's problems. Let me try to show it. I want to pick out the three great victories of which Paul speaks in this chapter, and to try to show what it means to say that Christ gives us the victory over sin, over death, and over the world.

(1) *Victory over sin.* What does that mean? Does it mean anything to the typical modern man? The very word 'sin' has a remote and unreal sound to a great many people today. It does not 'ring a bell'. Our Christian forefathers used to speak a great deal about the 'sense of sin' as something important. But to a vast number of people today it sounds like a piece of religious jargon and nothing more. It is often said that the typical modern man has an easy conscience and no

sense of sin; and therefore the central Christian message of the forgiveness of sins makes no appeal to him: he can hardly understand it. And yet, on the other hand, here is a very curious fact: according to the psycho-analysts and psychiatrists, one of the commonest symptoms of nervous trouble in our time is the 'guilt-feeling', the vague half-repressed and unaccountable sense of guilt. That is apparently something peculiarly characteristic of the modern world, a malady of our neurotic age.

Now, how can both of these things be true? What is the real situation? Something like this. I don't believe the morbid guilt-feeling is just the same thing as the Christian sense of sin. I believe it is a much less wholesome substitute for it, the kind of substitute that grows up in an age in which many people have lost the sense of God. There are so many serious-minded people today who have no lively faith in God. They still have a sense of moral responsibility. They can't give that up. And so they try to have morality without religion, without God. But that is too difficult. They don't know what to do with their failures, because they have no God to forgive them. So they can't face their failures. They unconsciously repress the memory of them. And repression is just what produces morbid complexes. And so they come to have the guilt-feeling. It doesn't do them any good, but rather paralyses moral endeavour. I believe a good deal of that is true not only of people definitely suffering from nervous trouble, but of many ordinary people today (perhaps some of ourselves) though they do not quite know it themselves.

What do these people need? They need to be made conscious of God, of the God and Father of our Lord Jesus Christ. Then their failures will look different. Then their guilt-feeling will be transformed into a sense of sin against God, betrayal of the love of God. That seems to make the

146

situation far worse than ever. Yes, but also far better than ever, because of the new and wonderful possibility of the divine forgiveness. When a man comes to believe in that, and to accept it, then he can forgive himself, and he finds release and a new beginning—indeed, a new beginning every day. That is the victory over sin in the daily discipline of the Christian life.

Now the New Testament constantly connects that with the death and resurrection of Christ. When God through Christ brings us to repentance and forgives us, then somehow the death and resurrection of Christ are reproduced in us. Our sins are buried with Christ, and we are given a new start, so that, as Paul puts it, we die to sin and live to God, we rise with Christ into newness of life. That is one of the great discoveries of the Christian Gospel: that we do not achieve the moral victory by a mere moral effort, but by casting ourselves on the grace of God, who through Christ forgives us the past and gives us the future. Trying to keep God's law seems only to strengthen the evil within us. That is why Paul here says: 'The power of sin is the law.' The Christian method is different, and better, and so Paul goes on: 'But thanks be to God, who gives us the victory, through our Lord Jesus Christ'—victory over sin.

(2) *Victory over death*. There is no doubt that the New Testament regards death as an enemy. And it doesn't try to conquer death by making light of it. It regards death as a dreadful reality. And I believe that something of that realism about death has come back into the thought and literature of our time, perhaps as a result of two world wars. Even young people today do not pretend to ignore death. It invades their minds as an inescapable problem. Not in the sense that they would be afraid to die themselves, but in the sense that this universal fate of death seems to set a great question-mark over everything. It is 'the last enemy'.

How can we have the victory over it? Is it by finding some proof of the immortality of the soul, either by philosophical arguments or by psychical research putting us into touch in occult ways with the spirits of the departed? In both of these ways the attempt has often been made to prove that, when the body dies, something called the soul continues to exist. But does that give us the victory over death? Suppose you could, by those methods, prove that after the death of the body something called the soul lasts on. Does that help us much? Does that tell us what we really need to know? If that were all that we could say, is it a very significant or a very inviting prospect? Nay, what we really want to know is whether human life has a meaning and purpose both on this side and on the other side of death, something that death cannot defeat. And that assurance can only come to us through faith and trust in God.

Do you remember how Jesus argued that since God called Himself the God of Abraham and of Isaac and of Jacob, and since He is not the God of the dead but of the living, therefore we may be sure that those men, though they died and were buried long ago, are not just dead, but are alive in God? That was Jesus' argument for immortality. It was all because of God. And then finally, when He passed through the gates of death Himself, He became the supreme instance of His own argument, and clinched it for ever. And His followers could now say: 'Blessed be (not the God of Abraham and Isaac and Jacob, but better still) the God and Father of our Lord Jesus Christ, who has begotten us again to a living hope by the resurrection of Jesus Christ from the dead.' And they said, in Paul's words, 'He that raised up the Lord Jesus will raise us up too'.

That is enough. That gives us what we need. Of course it does not answer all our questions about what lies beyond, but it gives us the victory over death. And we can leave the rest in God's hands, and say: 'Thanks be to God, who gives us the victory through our Lord Jesus Christ.'

(3) *Victory over the world.* What does that signify? I think a great many people today are oppressed with a sense of the meaninglessness of human existence; and especially young people. If only we could see that human life on earth through the centuries was leading to something! If only we could detect some direction and pattern and progress. But we can't. It is all chaos. The dreadful sense of meaninglessness is one of the troubles of our age.

But also, just in this age, and perhaps partly just because everything looks so hopeless, Christianity is rediscovering something which from the beginning was at the very heart of its message—the great hope, the sure conviction, of the ultimate victory of God's Kingdom. Christians all over the world are thinking of that in this particular year (1954), because it is to be the central subject of the great Assembly of the World Council of Churches in America in August: Christ the Hope of the World, through whom God is leading history on to a splendid consummation.

Now that is part of what Paul is thinking of when he thanks God for giving us the victory through Christ. It is a notable thing how, right in the middle of this long chapter about resurrection—Christ's resurrection and ours—Paul suddenly plunges into a remarkable passage about the splendid climax to which God is leading the whole universe, a kind of cosmic redemption in which all evil will be done away and God will be all in all. And what difference does it make to us if we believe in that? The answer is: it saves us from the sense of meaninglessness. For another notable thing about the chapter is that at the very end of his whole long argument Paul says just that. Just after thanking God for the victory, he says: 'Therefore, brothers, be stedfast, immovable, always abounding in the work of the Lord, because now you know that your labour is not in vain.' Don't you see? That is to say: 'because now you know that your work is not meaningless.'

In an age like the present, amid the clash of tragic forces in this mad world, most of us are sometimes tempted to give up our endeavours and to ask, Is it all worth while? Our endeavours to make our work significant as a contribution towards a better order of things—aren't they all sucked like drops into the ocean of chaos? Do they make any difference at all?

But if, through Christ, we believe in the purpose and victory of God, then meaninglessness is overcome, and we know that even our feeblest little endeavours to serve God and man in our daily callings are abundantly worth while. They are 'not in vain', they will not be wasted, they cannot be lost, because they are caught up and purified and blessed and used as part of the campaign of an invincible Kingdom whose victory is sure. Their meaninglessness is vanquished through Him who has overcome the world. And we can say again, 'Thanks be to God, who gives us the victory through our Lord Jesus Christ.'

19. LOW SUNDAY

But he himself went a day's journey into the wilderness, and came and sat down under a juniper tree; and he requested for himself that he might die; and said, It is enough; now, O Lord, take away my life; for I am not better than my fathers.   1 KINGS 19.4

THE Sunday after Easter is commonly called Low Sunday. It is not quite certain what the origin of this name is, but some have connected it with the familiar fact that in living the Christian life we sometimes pass from the mountain-top to the low valley. Easter Day, when we remember the victory that God has given us in Christ, is the high point of the whole Christian year; and because we cannot always remain on the heights, because moods change, and reactions come, and exaltation may be followed by depression, Easter Day is followed by Low Sunday.

But whether that has anything to do with the origin of the phrase or not, there is no doubt that for a great many people the Christian life does have these changes of mood and temper, those reactions, those bad hours. Therefore I think it may be useful today to consider for a little how we ought to deal with them. And that is why I have taken the story of Elijah under the juniper tree, utterly dejected and praying that he might die.

In the case of Elijah this did come just after the highest moment of his life, his triumph over the priests of Baal on Mount Carmel. That was indeed the victory of faith, and at the end of that chapter we find him dancing in prophetic ecstasy. And now, after the victory, comes the reaction, the depression, the doubt whether his work was of any value at all, and whether the cause of God had any future. We see him going off into the desert and throwing himself on the ground under a juniper tree, and saying: 'It is enough; now, O Lord, take away my life; for I am not better than my fathers.' That was his black hour. And that picture of Elijah under the juniper tree is a kind of timeless image and symbol of what so many of us experience now and again—of our times of depression, when the taste goes out of our life and out of our religion, when God becomes unreal and it is difficult to pray to Him or to enjoy Him.

What is the meaning of these moods? What ought we to think about them? How ought we to face them and deal with them?

To begin with, we must make sure that we have not, ourselves, created the cloud that is hiding God from our eyes. Perhaps we have created it by disobedience. Perhaps we are running away from God and from His will, and that is why we cannot enjoy the light of His countenance. Perhaps it is partly true even of Elijah that his gloom was due to his having run away into the wilderness, away from difficult duty, away from God's will. Anyway, God came and asked him: 'What are you doing here, Elijah?' And then God sent him back to where he had fled from, and told him what he had to do. But, whether this is quite true of Elijah or not, it is sometimes true of Christians that they are themselves to blame for their times of gloom, because they are running away from God. And before we go any further, we must make sure of that point and put right what is wrong.

But of course that is not always the reason. And having dealt with that, I want now to go on to give you some simple bits of encouragement and counsel for those times when you are under the shadow of the juniper tree.

(1) Remember that *this is part of the common experience of the Christian life.* You are not different from others. You are not the first. We have started from the case of Elijah,

away back in ancient Israel. But it is still more striking to note that this kind of experience is common right through the story of Christianity. It is indeed rather wonderful to discover how many of the great Christian saints and masters of the spiritual life tell of the times of dejection and desolation through which they passed. It has been so common an experience that it came to have special technical names attached to it. Sometimes it was called the experience of desolation (the opposite of consolation), and sometimes it was called 'spiritual dryness', because it felt so like being in a dry and thirsty desert where there are no springs of water. For example, St. Francis de Sales, after speaking of the fine weather of religious joyfulness, goes on:

> But this fine weather will not always continue; but sometimes you will find yourself so absolutely devoid of all feeling of devotion that your soul will seem to you to be a fruitless barren desert in which there is no pathway to find her God, nor any water of grace to refresh her, because of the dryness which seems to lay her entirely waste.

It is then a widespread and common experience, very familiar even to those saints and masters who have gone far beyond what most of us have ever attained in the practice of the Christian life. These masters tell us what to do with our bad moods, and I am coming to that in a moment. But meantime I think it is a real help to discover the mere fact that the experience of days of depression has always been a common one among Christians, and thus, as it were, to clasp hands across the centuries with others, with fellow-Christians of all generations, who have passed through it too. So I say: Remember that for your encouragement.

(2) Remember that *what really matters in the Christian life is not our feelings, our emotions, our moods, but how we live,* with dedicated wills, in faith and love. And thus we ought to be looking away from ourselves and our own feelings to God above us and our fellow-creatures around us. A great

many people make the mistake of judging their religious life by the state of their feelings, by whether they are enjoying it or not, whether they can always take delight in praying to God and worshipping Him. And so, when they experience bad hours, in which God seems far away and all inspiration and joy seem to have departed, they are unduly discouraged. But that is really an elementary mistake. That is not the way to deal with our moods. Our feelings are bound to change. Our moods are sure to vary, just like the weather. But the Christian life must go on, independently of all the variations in the weather of our souls.

Of course there ought to be also in our Christian lives the days of a clear sky and the divine sunshine. But it is not by concentrating on ourselves and our feelings that we shall get the weather of the soul to come right in that respect. No, it is rather by forgetting ourselves, and performing our routine duties. What a blessing it is that in our uninspired hours there are the hum-drum duties that can be faithfully carried out without inspiration, and our fellow-men around us to whom we can be loyal and considerate even when we are depressed ourselves. But above all, let us remind ourselves that the great reality of God does not change with our changing moods. Even if at certain moments we cannot feel His presence, we do believe in His unchanging reality, in His eternal love, in what He has done for us through Christ, in His unfailing purpose of good. If we keep firm hold of these great realities, or rather let them keep firm hold of us, yielding our wills to God's will, then our feelings and emotions will take care of themselves. Or rather, God will give us such feelings, of consolation or desolation, as are good for us. He does not change. He is there, in all His blessed reality, behind the clouds that hide Him. He may be very near us just in those hours when we cannot feel His presence at all.

(3) In your bad hours, remember the *fellowship of your*

fellow Christians, and lean upon it. That is half the meaning of the Church of Christ. We are far too apt to live the Christian life in a kind of proud loneliness and independence, with a 'lone-wolf' kind of religion. But that is not what Christianity was ever meant to be. That is not how Christian gladness, as you find it in the New Testament, is generated. From the beginning Christianity was a rich and warm fellowship, and its joy was the joy of a beloved community. While you are walking by yourself in lonely brooding, there are doubtless others around you doing the same. And how much you could help them and they could help you if you took more seriously the comfort of the fellowship that ought to exist in the Church of Christ!

When Elijah lay under the juniper tree, in the depths of depression, he thought he was the only faithful Israelite left who had not fallen away to worship false gods. But God told him: 'I have yet seven thousand in Israel who have not bowed the knee to Baal', and he sent Elijah back into the service and fellowship of that church of the faithful. And God speaks to us in our depression and tells us to get away from lonely brooding into that mutual sharing of burdens and responsibilities, of joys and sorrows, of thought and worship, which is the very life of the Church of Christ, where 'brother clasps the hand of brother, stepping fearless through the night'.

I want to sum all this up by reminding you of a splendid passage in the *Pilgrim's Progress*, where Bunyan deals in his allegorical way with exactly the situation we are considering this morning; and undoubtedly he is drawing upon his own experience. I mean the passage about Christian the pilgrim going through the valley of the shadow of death. When Bunyan put that into his allegory he was not thinking of the actual death of the Christian, but of the experience of spiritual darkness, through which many a Christian has sometimes to pass. As the pilgrim was passing through this dark valley groping his way, he became so confused that he did not know the sound of his own voice, and when an evil spirit jumped on his shoulder and whispered blasphemous thoughts into his ear, he thought they came from his own mind. He was utterly disconsolate. And now comes this passage:

When Christian had travelled in this disconsolate condition some considerable time, he thought he heard the voice of a man, as going before him, saying:'Though I walk through the Valley of the Shadow of Death, I will fear none ill, for Thou art with me.' Then he was glad and that for three reasons.

First, because he gathered from thence that some who feared God were in this valley as well as himself.

Secondly, for that he perceived God was with them, though in that dark and dismal state; and why not, he thought, with me, though by reason of the impediment that attends this place, I cannot perceive it?

Thirdly, for that he hoped, could he overtake them, to have company by and by. So he went on, and called to him that was before; but he knew not what to answer for that he also thought himself to be alone. And by and by the day broke; then said Christian: 'He hath turned the shadow of death into the morning.'

Yes, the morning comes. The dark night of the soul does not last for ever. And so, while it lasts, we can say to ourselves in the words of another ancient Psalmist:

> Why art thou cast down, O my soul?
> And why art thou disquieted within me?
> Hope thou in God, for I shall yet praise Him,
> Who is the health of my countenance and my God.

And now unto God the Father, God the Son, and God the Holy Ghost, be ascribed in the Church, as is most justly due, all honour, glory, might, majesty, dominion and blessing, world without end.

III

SERMONS ON VARIOUS OCCASIONS

20. THE MANIFOLD GRACE OF GOD

[Preached before Cambridge University Ecumenical Association, 1949]

As every man hath received the gift, even so minister the same one to another as good stewards of the manifold grace of God. I PETER 4.10

A VAST number of Christians today are gravely concerned about the divided state of the Church; and the Ecumenical Movement, which is such a remarkable and exhilarating phenomenon in the life of our age, has made the problem appear more acute and tragic than ever, because even when we are drawn together in great ecumenical assemblies and realize our unity in Christ, we cannot all meet together as communicants at the Lord's Table.

Sometimes in our discussions of the matters that keep us apart we are tempted to conclude that there is an impassable gulf between those who would call themselves Catholics on the one hand and those who would call themselves Protestants or Evangelicals on the other, because they have utterly irreconcilable conceptions of the nature of the Church and its Sacraments. Sometimes we are tempted to suggest that when these two groups speak of the Sacrament of Holy Communion, they are talking of two different things, so that the very idea of inter-communion between the Churches would be artificial.

But I cannot believe this to be true. At the Amsterdam Assembly when I was taking part in the discussions, in one of its Sections, about the nature of the Church, I was repeatedly struck by the fact that it was much easier to define our agreements than to define our differences. Of course there were some wide divergences, since we were gathered from almost every kind of Church in the world except the Roman. But it became clear that the facts would not fall neatly into the antithesis between Catholic and Protestant or Evangelical. And it was partly because when either party tried to formulate the difference of belief, representatives of the other party sometimes felt disposed to say: 'No, we cannot accept that formulation, because we believe much of what you claim as yours, and what you have said about our position does not describe it as we should describe it.' The 'Catholic' is bent upon emphasizing the givenness of the Church, and its continuity, on what we may call the horizontal plane, with the Church of the Apostles and the historical Incarnation. But the Protestants believe in that too. Again, the 'Protestant' insists upon the present vertical relation of the Church, by faith, to the Living and Exalted Christ, who constitutes His Church in every age. But, then, so does the 'Catholic'. So it seems far easier to agree upon the formulation of our agreements than to agree upon the formulation of our differences. And that ironical fact, that baffling discovery, surely has its hopeful and encouraging aspect. For it suggests that if we could all go deeper still into our theological foundations, we might find ourselves nearer to each other than we realized or expected.

There is one conception in particular that seems to me to offer a hopeful basis of mutual understanding. It is that which is mentioned in our text, and which must obviously be fundamental in the discussion of these matters: the conception of the grace of God. Church and Sacraments are, above all else, means of grace, channels and instruments of grace, and all that happens in and through them is wrought by 'the manifold grace of God'. So our whole understanding of Church, Ministry and Sacraments must be bound up with the question, What is grace? What do we mean by the grace of God?

Now it appears to me that within the last generation there has been a certain advance in the theological elucidation of this concept of grace; and, moreover, it is an advance in which Catholics and Evangelicals, Anglicans and Presbyterians, seem to be marching in step with each other. The advance and the agreement may be roughly summed up in this way: we have come to see more clearly that grace must not be conceived as anything like an impersonal force or substance or quantity, impinging upon the human soul or poured into it, but wholly as a personal relationship. It is God's gracious personal influence on men.

My first witness will be from the Anglican side: the late Professor N. P. Williams of Oxford, who would certainly have called himself a Catholic. In his admirable little book *The Grace of God* he pointed out that from the third century onwards, and right through the Middle Ages the doctrine of grace had been somewhat beset by an impersonal conception (Aquinas called it 'a supernatural somewhat'). As against all such ideas Williams went great lengths in maintaining that the work of grace is nothing other than the direct personal action of the Holy Spirit upon the human heart. A precisely parallel line of thought was pursued independently by that eminent Presbyterian divine whose praises it is unnecessary to sing in Cambridge, the late Principal John Oman. In his book *Grace and Personality* he worked out the conception of the grace of God as 'a gracious personal relationship' on the analogy of the relation between a father and his child, and maintained that many of the problems, as old as St. Augustine, concerning the relation between divine grace and human personality become tractable in a new way when we begin to think of grace in those personal categories.

Another impressive witness from the Anglican side is Professor Leonard Hodgson of Oxford. He warns us against conceiving of grace as something detachable from God's living personal activity, like the medicine which helps a patient between the doctor's visits; or something magical, like the love-potions by which a lover sought to influence a girl to love him; or something mechanical, like an electric current transmitted through a cable. As against all those utterly false conceptions, he reminds us that the grace we receive in the Sacrament is the power that comes into human life through personal communion with a Person. Let me quote one more Anglican divine (for I am specially glad to bring witnesses from that quarter). Dr Oscar Hardmann tells us that grace 'is not a commodity which is conveyed into man's being for the healing and rehabilitation of his nature; but it is the power of the Personality of the Creator working upon the personality of each of His creatures by the means which we commonly describe as personal influence.'

It may be said that there is nothing particularly novel about all this. But what strikes me as impressive is that we have here a new and notable agreement between thinkers of very different traditions about how we are to think of the grace of God. It is indeed very much in line with the re-discovery of the Pauline idea of grace which was claimed by the Reformers of the sixteenth century. But it goes further, and represents a real development of thought in the twentieth century, which sheds a new light on some very old problems for both Catholics and Protestants by coming to understand grace as a living personal relationship between God and Man.

Now let us apply that to the problem of the sacramental order in the Church. One of the divisive questions is that of the nature of the Church's continuity through the centuries. But we are all agreed that the continuity itself is important. The Christian religion is not a system of timeless truths through which the individual can enter into a mystical union with God: it is an historical faith, centring on an actual episode in the distant past, the Incarnation of the Divine Word in Jesus of Nazareth. That episode could not last for ever: it was quickly over. What then could it accomplish for the generations and centuries that were to follow, unless some channel could be created by which the new thing that had come into the world could be made available for future ages? The channel that was created is the Church; and so far, we are all agreed. But when we come to define the nature of its continuity, we seem to find agreement much more difficult.

What I wish to suggest is that in this very matter the conception of grace as a personal relationship brings us closer together than we have yet realized.

If grace is a personal relationship between God and man, then we cannot allow ourselves ever to think of it as a stream that has to flow down the centuries from a source in the distant past through the channel of a sacramental system. We all know that quite well. But how easy it is to fall back unawares into the crude conception: as if the Church were a kind of installation by which the grace that entered the world with the Incarnation continues to flow through history like a stream of oil through a pipe-line or like an electric current through a cable! From that point of view the continuity of the Church would mean that the pipe-line has never been broken, the cable has never been cut. If it had been, the stream of supernatural grace would have been lost beyond recapture. But we all realize how preposterous these ideas are. They would imply that grace was something left behind by Christ when He died, to be stored up because He is dead. And so we have a dead Christ in the distant past. But all that makes nonsense if grace is a personal relationship. Then we are not concerned with a dead Christ in the distant past, whose grace has to come to us across the centuries, but with a living Christ, who lives in His Church here and now in a gracious personal relation with us. And all that we say about Church and Ministry and Sacraments must be said in the light of that.

And what then of the historical continuity? That question is not now difficult to answer. For the vertical relation to the Living Christ can never be independent of the horizontal relationship to the historical Incarnation. It is through the Gospel of the Word-made-flesh, interpreted by the witness of the Church in Word and Sacrament, that God gives His grace to men in every age and the Holy Spirit does His work. And the continuity of the Church from age to age in an orderly succession is all-important: not because the grace of God flows down the centuries as it were through the finger-tips of ordaining bishops or presbyters, but because the authentic treasure of the Gospel must be preserved. That continuity is but the servant of a still more vital continuity, not with the past, but with the Unseen: the continuity here and now between the Church on earth and the Church in heaven; and, above all, that continuity, that personal relationship between the Church on earth and its Lord in heaven, which is but another name for the grace of God.

In a similar way the extreme opposite views of the meaning of Holy Communion come much nearer to each other when we view them in the light of that conception of grace. Is the Sacrament merely a memorial feast in which we commemorate an event in the distant past? Or is it a eucharistic sacrifice in which in every celebration we take part? That is a simple and highly controversial antithesis. And yet in the light of the personal conception of grace we can see that it is *too* neat and simple. If grace is really a personal relationship, then the Sacrament cannot be merely a commemoration, as if Christ were merely past and not present. And again, as we shall all agree, it cannot be a repetition of the ancient sacrifice on Calvary. That we cannot repeat. And we do not need to add to it. For the sacrifice of the Lamb of God is in some sense an eternal sacrifice, being continually offered on the heavenly altar in a divine sin-bearing which never ends. And in the

Sacrament we do not merely recall it to our remembrance, but also make a memorial of it before God, uniting ourselves with it by faith and pleading its benefits, that we may obtain mercy and find grace. If we can all say these things together, we are not so far apart as we often imagine.

It is always foolish to gloss over our disagreements. But it is even more foolish to exaggerate them. And I am urging that even in these controversial matters we can go a very long way together when we realize what we really mean by 'the manifold grace of God'.

21. SCIENCE AND RELIGION

[Sermon Delivered in St. Giles Cathedral, Edinburgh, before the British Association for the Advancement of Science, on 12th August, 1951]

In that same hour Jesus rejoiced in the Holy Spirit and said: I thank thee, O Father, Lord of heaven and earth, that thou hast concealed these things from the wise and understanding, and hast revealed them unto babes. Even so, Father, for so it seemed good in thy sight.

LUKE 10.21

IT is a commonplace to say that there is much less talk than there used to be about the conflict between science and religion. This does not mean that there is no longer any kind of conflict, but rather perhaps that the conflict is at a deeper level. At certain periods in the lives of our fathers and grand-fathers it was commonly supposed to be a conflict between some particular conclusions of modern science and some traditional dogmas of Christianity. But now it appears rather as a struggle between two different habits of mind, a psychological conflict between two diverse ways of approaching the problem of truth and reality. The one habit might conveniently be symbolized by the familiar phrase 'the scientific conscience', and the other by the equally famous phrase 'the will to believe'.

But again: it seems to me that the most significant part of this conflict is not between the scientists and the theologians as two different sets of people, but rather between two diverse tendencies in the same person, two parts of one man—between the scientist and the theologian which may exist in the same human breast. It is a tension in the mind of the intellectual between the honest consideration of evidence on the one hand and the haunting claims of faith on the other. In this scientific age, the mind which has become habituated to the empirical methods of natural science may almost unconsciously become conditioned into an attitude which distrusts any other way of attaining truth; and so the conflict arises. Moreover, in our own time this conflict has assumed a more subtle and painful form than ever through some of the newer developments of psychology. Modern psychology has shown us that we are much less rational beings than we used to imagine, and that our opinions and beliefs are continually at the mercy of unconscious motives, escape-mechanisms, phantasies, projections, wishful thinking. In some quarters these psychological discoveries have been used to the disadvantage of religious belief, explaining it away in the most desolating manner. And so in many minds the conflict tends to take the form of a meticulous dread of wishful thinking, a self-questioning as to whether one's religion is anything more than an escape into phantasy, or one's God anything more than a projection. And this conflicts with that devout persuasion in our hearts, deeper than all proofs and arguments, which tells us about God and the meaning of life, that intuitive movement of the human spirit which William James more than half a century ago somewhat dangerously designated 'the will to believe'.

Thus the intellectual may be torn between two opposite temptations: on the one hand the temptation to be very chary and non-committal about all religious belief, because of his scientific (or we might say his psychological) conscience, and on the other hand the temptation to flee from his scientific conscience altogether, with a certain dishonesty, because he is afraid of straining his faith in God. Moreover, it is not a quite simple and easy matter to overcome that tension. It is a deep and genuine tension. For on the one hand, it is quite true that we are prone to wishful thinking, and there is a real danger of our religion becoming an escape into a world of phantasy in which we unconsciously will to believe. Yes, but on the other hand there is such a thing as the will to *dis*believe, and it may even masquerade under the disguise of the scientific conscience. Unbelief itself may be an escape-mechanism, a running away from reality; so that we may have to psycho-analyse our scepticism as well as our religious faith. We are indeed 'fearfully and wonderfully made', with minds whose mysterious twistings we do not ourselves understand. If only we could learn the humility and honesty of a mind which is really committed and dedicated, with the veracity of the scientific conscience and the receptiveness of the will-to-believe united in what can only be described as the child-like heart!

Now that is precisely the spirit whose blessings are celebrated in those golden words of Christ's which I announced as my text: words which surely ought to be laid up in the hearts of all who are engaged in intellectual pursuits, whether they are teachers or students, whether they are scientists or humanists, philosophers or theologians. 'In that same hour Jesus rejoiced in the Holy Spirit and said: I thank thee, O Father, Lord of heaven and earth, that thou hast concealed these things from the wise and understanding, (we might almost translate "from the intelligentsia") and hast revealed them unto babes. Even so, Father, for so it seemed good in thy sight.' Needless to say, this is not to be taken as a disfranchisement of the true intellectuals in religious matters, as if it were better not to have a fine intellect or not to use or train it; but rather as an *en*franchisement of the *un*intellectual who have the innocence of the eye and of the mind. But it also gives a profound and positive message to all and sundry about the real road to the understanding of divine mysteries.

One of the key words in this passage is the word 'revealed'. And this surely is one of the most important things ever said about the nature and meaning of revelation. What is

revelation? Is there such a thing as 'revealed' knowl[...]
antithesis to natural knowledge? And if so, how [...]
come? Jesus here tells us that the deepest mysterie[...]
universe, which remain hidden from those who trust merely
in their own acumen, are revealed to babes. That means,
surely, to those who have the childlike heart. They may be
highly intellectual, or they may not. They may be members
of what we call the intelligentsia, or they may not. But they
are simple-hearted and honest, with something of the wide-
open eyes of little children gazing at reality. Their minds are
not sophisticated by pride, but are obedient and dedicated.
And it is to such minds that the deepest things are revealed.
There are many kinds of natural knowledge which demand
only mental acumen from the learner, though it may well be
that even scientific knowledge at its best and highest requires
something more. But it is quite certain that the knowledge
of God comes in a different way altogether. It is an assurance,
an understanding, a revelation, given to humble honest
obedient hearts. That is how the universe discloses its most
vital secrets. And in this passage Jesus rejoices that it is so.
He gives thanks to God Almighty, the Maker of heaven and
earth, that He has built and ordered His universe in such a
way that its deepest mysteries, which may be hidden from
the intellectuals, are 'revealed unto babes'. 'Even so, Father,
for so it seemed good in thy sight.'

There are two fatal misunderstandings of this truth, against
which we must warn ourselves.

(1) In the first place, it must not be taken to mean that
we ought to paralyse or destroy our intellectual life in order
to be able to accept the dogmas of religion. When we use
the famous and noble phrase *sacrificium intellectus*, 'sacrifice
of the intellect', we must remind ourselves that 'sacrifice' in
its truly religious sense does not mean destruction but oblation
or offering to God. And the offering must be an unblemished

one, free from all blemish of intellectual dishonesty, the dedication of the whole mind to God, who is the Truth.

(2) But the other misunderstanding is much more subtle and dangerous. The principle laid down in our text might be taken to suggest that while religious belief is natural and easy for simple souls, it can hardly be expected, in any very definite commitment, in the case of intellectuals. That is not a purely imaginary misunderstanding. Indeed that attitude has sometimes been fairly common among high-minded intellectuals. They had a lively scientific conscience, they were conscious of the difficulties of religious belief. They were far from being scornful or unsympathetic, they perhaps had genuine devout sentiments, and great respect for those whose faith was clear. They would perhaps even say that the great assertions of the Christian Gospel might very well be true. But for themselves, they hardly expected to get so far as that, because an intellectual is bound to be specially conscious of the difficulties of belief, and to hold his judgment in suspense; perhaps giving his blessing to Christianity, but with an air of high-minded agnosticism. Let other people have their religious faith and practice, but the intellectual is doomed to be content with something less, and to remain uncommitted.

Surely it is plain that there is something sadly wrong-headed about such an attitude when it is accepted as final, as something with which to be content. It contains a deep self-contradiction. For, after all, if Christianity is true, it must be vastly important. And so it must be vastly important for any man to know whether it is true. Moreover, it must be possible to know—at least to know sufficiently for our daily needs. To suggest that belief is only for simple souls, and that intellectuals cannot be expected to reach it, is to suggest that God has ordered His universe in such an odd and churlish way that those whom He has most richly endowed with intellectual gifts are thereby disqualified for seeking and finding Him, or at least gravely handicapped in the quest. But if God is like that, Christianity is not true. If Christianity is true, God is infinitely gracious and compassionate in His quest of man. He has not left us in the dark, but has done everything that could be done, to the point of becoming incarnate and bearing the sins and sorrows of the world on Calvary, to reveal Himself to men, with the promise that those who seek Him shall find Him. So, if the truth is anything like that, it must be available to those who are really willing to seek it. And therefore, however great the difficulties of belief may be to sincere and honest souls (and far be it from me to speak of these difficulties with anything but respect and sympathy), yet nothing can be more unreasonable than the attitude of those who are content to be *benevolent spectators*, pursuing the truth only in an otiose and uncommitted way, hardly expecting to find anything positive; as if life could wait indefinitely, and almost as if genuine seeking and finding and believing did not greatly matter.

I will bring these reflections to a close by quoting to you two searching utterances from the pens of two notable seekers after truth.

The first is from one of our own contemporaries, that imaginative genius Katherine Mansfield, written in a letter not long before she died so young.

I am so sick of all this modern seeking which ends in seeking. Seek by all means, but the text goes on 'and ye shall find'. And although of course there can be no ultimate finding, there is a kind of finding by the way which is enough, is sufficient. But these seekers in the looking-glass, these half-female frightened writers of today— you know, they remind me of the green-fly in roses, they are a kind of blight.

Don't these words, written by a desperately sincere intellectual, expose an unwholesome habit of mind which many of us can detect in germ in ourselves, and which may indeed be a blight in the world of thought; a habit which savours of the sentimentalism of dramatizing oneself as a superior kind of person who prefers wandering and wondering to finding and believing, and is content to remain without any ultimate commitment or allegiance. But a man cannot live on that cult of uncertainty; and if we choose to try, we may even lose both the scientific conscience and the will to believe, because we have lost the childlike heart.

So I will conclude by quoting this other utterance, left behind him by one who was both one of the great seekers and one of the great scientists of the ages, Blaise Pascal. He said:

> There are only two kinds of people who can be called reasonable: those who serve God with all their hearts because they know Him; and those who seek Him with all their hearts because they do not know Him yet.

22. TO MAKE READY A PEOPLE

[Sermon preached before the Conference on Faith and Order
in Lund, Sweden, in August, 1952]

To make ready a people prepared for the Lord.
LUKE 1.17

THAT beloved Scottish preacher of the days of my youth,
John Kelman, began his book on his travels in Palestine with
this sentence: 'A journey through the Holy Land may reason-
ably be expected to be in some sort a sacramental experience
in a man's life.' But he knew very well how misleading and
dangerous such an expectation may be. On the third page
he goes on to speak of the people who expect to find in the
sacred sites of the Holy Land some occult and magical qualities which would in themselves communicate a revelation.
He takes the notable example of Pierre Loti, who went to
Palestine with the hope that some experience might there be
given him which would revive his lost faith in Christianity.
Loti was bitterly disappointed and disillusioned. And finally,
he tells us, in the Garden of Gethsemane, he stood beating
his brow in the darkness against the stem of an olive-tree,
waiting for something to happen. But nothing happened.
There was no revelation. And he cried in despair: 'No, there
is nothing. No one sees me. No one answers me.' In the
landscapes of Palestine, even though they were the scene and
setting of the Word-made-flesh, there was nothing that
could speak to one who did not bring a mind made ready by
faith and prepared for the Lord.

A visit to the Holy Land is not a sacrament at all, and in
the proper sense perhaps should not even be called sacramental. And yet we have here an extraordinarily good

173

parable of what is true even of the Sacraments of the Gospel. And that is why, looking forward to the celebration of Holy Communion tomorrow morning, we are here tonight for a service of preparation.

It is a common experience for Christians to come to a Communion service and find that their hearts cannot rise to the height of the occasion. The familiar sacred words are spoken, the bread is broken and the wine is poured out, and they receive the elements. But they are unable to lift up their hearts unto the Lord. The hour passes, and they go away, with the sense that they have not opened their hearts to the grace of God or offered the sacrifice of thanksgiving. Now, it may very well be that they are making the elementary mistake of taking their momentary emotions as the test of their worship. It may be that though they had no sense of enjoying the presence of God, He was feeding them with bread from heaven. But it may also be that the Sacrament was not truly sacramental to them because they did not receive it in faith, since, as St. Augustine said, we cannot carry away from the Sacrament more than we can collect in the vessel of faith. And it may be that the reason why their faith was dormant and sluggish, and even perhaps their attention wandering, was because they had not taken the trouble to prepare themselves for the Sacrament, that they might come to it 'made ready as a people prepared for the Lord'.

But why should we have to prepare ourselves beforehand for what is intended in itself to be to us a means of grace? To speak of preparing our hearts for it may seem to suggest that the Sacrament depends on us, on our subjective frame of mind, on our being able to induce the appropriate thoughts and feelings. Whereas the very meaning of a Sacrament is that God is waiting to be gracious to us, with a prevenient grace which does not depend upon us, and with supernatural gifts which only He can give and we can only receive. Yes, indeed. God has given us this Sacrament to enable us to look away from ourselves to Him, not gazing inwards upon our own souls, but outwards upon His grace and mercy and peace, which are as near and as real as the bread that is placed in our hands. And even the faith by which we receive these gifts is not of our making, but is His gift bestowed on our empty hands.

But even God's greatest gifts, even His own comings to us—do they call for no preparation? When God Himself, once for all, came right into our human situation, to visit and redeem His people in the Word-made-flesh, did He come without a call for preparation? Nay, the beautiful words which I announced as my text would never have been written if it had not been necessary to make preparation for that greatest of all divine comings, 'to make ready a people prepared for the Lord'. The words were spoken with reference to the mission of John the Baptist. And is it not a very notable thing that the four Gospels all take that mission of John as their starting-point in telling the story of the Ministry of Jesus? That was indeed 'the beginning of the Gospel of Jesus Christ'. The story could not be told without that beginning, and it is uniformly regarded by the evangelists as a divinely appointed *preparation* for Christ. Even when God visited and redeemed His people in the Word-made-flesh, in that central and living Sacrament which is Jesus Christ Himself, a preparation was needed—'to prepare in the desert a highway for our God,' to 'make ready a people prepared for the Lord.' That is how God works; and it is not strange that the Church has always called its members to prepare themselves for the Sacrament of the Lord's Supper.

But these words of our text carry us further, and suggest in three ways the kind of preparation we ought to be making tonight.

(1) In the first place, it ought to be an act of *penitence*. The preparation for Christ's coming in the flesh was a baptism of repentance. That was how John became a fore-runner to prepare the way of the Lord. And so it must be with us as we prepare for the Lord's Supper. I said a moment ago that when we celebrate the Sacrament we should not have our eyes turned inwards upon ourselves, but outward towards God. 'Lift up your hearts.' 'We lift them up unto the Lord.' That is indeed what we must do when we come to His Table: the sacred symbols must draw our gaze away from ourselves to Christ in all the reality of His love and power. Yes, but if we are to look away from ourselves *then*, we must look at ourselves *now*. 'Let a man examine himself,' says St. Paul, 'and so let him eat of that bread and drink of that cup'; and now is the time for that humble and penitent self-examina-tion. 'Humble yourselves therefore under the mighty hand of God, that in due time he may lift you up.' And now in this time of preparation, this eve of the Lord's Day, we must in His holy and gracious presence humble our hearts in contrition and repentance for our sins, in order that, when the time comes at the Holy Table tomorrow morning, we may be able to lift them up unto the Lord.

(2) In the second place, our text reminds us that our preparation of repentance is not only individual but *corporate*: 'to make ready *a people* prepared for the Lord.' A people. The whole plot of the story of God's redemptive work among men, as it is told in the Bible, is concerned not with isolated individuals, but with a people. In the Old Testament it was the people of Israel, that was a people for God's own posses-sion, chosen by Him to be His servant and to show forth His glory in the world. In the New Testament it was no less a people, the New Israel of God, the Church of Christ. God 'visited and redeemed His people,' calling men and women of every tribe and tongue and people and nation to be a chosen

race, a holy nation, a peculiar people, a kingdom of priests in His service—the Church of Christ.

Does He not then deal with us as individuals? Yes, indeed, He does. He seeks out each one of us for our salvation. But the very thing from which we need to be saved is the self-centred individualism which separates us, each one, from God and man, and which is the essence of sin. We need to be saved from our selfish isolated selves. And God saves us by calling us back into community with Himself and with our fellows through that redeemed community which is the Body of Christ, His Church, and which keeps the Festival of His broken Body.

We must indeed, each one for himself, make preparation for the Sacrament in the secret place of our inner chamber, in the presence of the Father who sees in secret; and that is what we are so often tempted to neglect. But when tomorrow we come to God's heavenly altar, we shall compass it as a people, a kingdom of priests, to make our corporate sacrifice of thanksgiving to God. And we must come 'made ready *as a people* prepared for the Lord,' with one heart and with one soul. And in order that we may be able to do it, we are here together tonight to make our corporate act of preparation and repentance.

But these two things that I have said become far more significant when we put them together, and then they lead to a third:

(3) In the third place, our penitence on this occasion must be above all else an act of *penitence for the divided state of the Church of Christ*, for our separation from one another.

How can we be 'made ready as a people prepared for the Lord' when we are divided, separated from each other? How can we be a people for God's own possession when we are not a people, but a variety of sects which cannot all even meet as communicants at the Lord's Table? Surely, then this must be a dominant note of our preparation tonight for our Communion tomorrow—the note of repentance for our breach of the unity of the body of Christ. That is something upon which we can all agree. Not one of us wishes to be disloyal to the traditions of our past. Not one of us would forget that when our forefathers separated from each other they did it in obedience to what they believed to be the demands of truth. Not one of us would wish to reduce the infinite variety of Christian truth and life to a barren uniformity. And not one of us will pretend that the problem of the reunion of the Church is a simple problem, or that the way forward is a perfectly plain path. But we shall all agree that there is something deeply tragic and sinful in the present divided state of the Church; and that we cannot wash our hands of responsibility for the blindness and narrowness, the pride and jealousy, the lack of charity and of zeal for the Kingdom of Christ, which have resulted from our divisions and which are helping men now to perpetuate them.

If these things are true, then what better can we do tonight than make an act of penitence together for the things that separate us from each other? It may be that because of our divisions some are looking forward with a certain amount of perplexity and anxiety to that great service tomorrow in which so many persons of widely diverse traditions will be united at the Lord's Table. But how can we better prepare for it than by asking God to turn our anxiety, which separates us, into the true contrition and forgiveness which can unite us; not the sorrow of the world, which worketh death, but the godly sorrow which is unto repentance and salvation? And then as we look forward to tomorrow, we can pray this other prayer:

O send out thy light and thy truth; let them lead us, let them bring us unto thy holy hill and to thy tabernacles. Then will we go unto the altar of God, unto God our exceeding joy. . . . For we shall yet praise him, who is the health of our countenance, and our God.

To Him be glory, both now and ever. AMEN.

Almighty God, Father of our Lord Jesus Christ, who hast set us in the Church of Thy dear Son, blessed be Thy name for our fellowship and unity in Him. Make us truly penitent for all that unworthily separates us from each other. As we now bow in silence before Thee, grant us, we beseech Thee, that spirit of humble contrition which Thou delightest to bless; and grant us likewise forgiveness and light and hope and peace. Through the same Jesus Christ our Lord. AMEN.

23. ELECTION

[Sermon preached in Manchester Cathedral, 1953]

And Jesus, walking by the sea of Galilee, saw two brethren, Simon called Peter, and Andrew his brother, casting a net into the sea: for they were fishers. And he saith unto them, Follow me, and I will make you fishers of men. And they straightway left their nets and followed him.
MATTHEW 4.18-20

I CHOOSE these words because this is St. Andrew's Eve. To me, as a Scotsman, coming from a country whose patron saint is St. Andrew and even from a city whose patron saint is St. Andrew, it is a great privilege to preach on St. Andrew's Eve in Manchester Cathedral. But I would be misusing the opportunity if I were to preach on distinctively Scottish interests, for St. Andrew belongs to all Christendom. I want to try to do something more universal: I want to speak quite simply about the doctrine of Election. People sometimes imagine that even that is a peculiarly Scottish and Calvinistic doctrine, and that in Scotland thoughtful people are going about most of the time discussing the mysteries of divine Predestination. I am afraid that is not true! But in any case the doctrine of Election, properly understood, belongs to all Christians, and lies at the very heart of the Gospel. It is quite a practical doctrine, and it concerns every one of us. It stands for something which ought to come home to our individual hearts every time we read or hear this story of Jesus calling Andrew by the Sea of Galilee.

In my dining-room at home there hangs a picture by the Scottish painter Sir David Wilkie, entitled 'The Reading of the Will'. A family lawyer is sitting at a table, with his spectacles on his nose and a scroll of parchment unrolled before him. Around him are gathered half-a-dozen persons, leaning forward towards him, straining their eyes and ears, including one old fellow who has an ear-trumpet, directed towards the voice of the lawyer. Their attention is riveted on the lawyer, they are hanging on his words, their faces are keen with interest—so different from what we so often look like when we are sitting in a pew during a sermon in church! Why are they listening so keenly? It is because a will is being read, the 'last will and testament' of some relative, in which they should have some share, and they are eagerly listening for their own names. Why do we listen in such a different way when the message of the New Testament is being read or preached? For this book also is a will and testament—the New Testament of our Lord and Saviour Jesus Christ. And surely when we read it or hear it read or expounded, we ought in a very true sense to be listening intently that we may hear our own names. Sometimes we do hear them. The Word speaks to our own hearts, almost as if our names were mentioned. When we are told the story of Christ calling the disciples by the Sea of Galilee, we suddenly hear Him calling us. It is as if our own names stood there in the will that is being read out, calling us to accept our inheritance in Christ. And that is how it ought to be, that is what ought to be expected in all the reading and hearing of the Word of God.

But can that happen to everybody? Does God choose and call everybody? Doesn't the Bible speak of 'those whose names from the foundation of the world are written in the Lamb's book of life?' Does that mean that some people's names are not written there? And what then? Doesn't this mean that some people are elect and some are not, so that it is taken out of our hands altogether? Isn't that the very meaning of the doctrine of Election? And yet—doesn't the New Testament also offer salvation freely to everybody, and say: 'Whosoever will, let him come'? How can we reconcile these things with each other? These are staggering questions, and no wonder people have sometimes revolted against the whole idea of divine Election. Some of these questions we perhaps cannot answer at all. But I want to use the story of the call to Andrew to suggest some simple thoughts that may help us to see what Election means. I want to say four things.

(1) *God always chooses us before we choose Him.* Surely that is true. Christ says to His disciples on the eve of His crucifixion: 'You did not choose me, but I chose you', and surely every true disciple would echo that, and say 'Yes'. Andrew was in his boat by the Sea of Galilee one day, when this Jesus came and said 'Follow me'. That was how it all began. And doesn't it always begin with God, who is always beforehand with us? The initiative is always His. And if you want to choose Christ, you may be sure that it is He that has moved you, because He chose you first. And Election means choosing.

We speak a great deal nowadays about man seeking God, and we sometimes picture the whole of human history as a process of mankind eagerly seeking God and gradually finding Him. Well, the Bible does speak of man seeking God. But it speaks far more of God seeking men, and sometimes seeking them against their wills and calling them. You can think of one after another of the great men of the Bible, and you will find that that is how it was with them: Moses, Gideon, Isaiah, Jeremiah, Saul of Tarsus. God came upon them unawares, and they shrank from His call at first, but ever afterwards they acknowledged that God had marked them out and called them, and they had to obey. They would never have sought Him if He had not first chosen them. And if you are seeking God, it is He who is making you do so. He has chosen you and called you. That is the divine Election.

(2) *God does not choose us because we deserve it.* He does

ELECTION

not choose us because we are more worthy of it than other
people, or because of anything good that He sees in us. That
is the reverse of the true order. Anything that is good in us
comes from Him, and His calling of us is sheer unmerited
grace and love.

Do we really believe that? At first it is difficult to accept,
and indeed this is what has sometimes made people want to
turn away from the doctrine of Election altogether. It seems
so capricious and arbitrary that God should choose people
quite regardless of their merits or demerits. Perhaps you
would say that when Christ called Andrew He must have
chosen him because of some good qualities He saw in him.
But I can't imagine Andrew himself or any of his fellow-
disciples, or any true Christian, saying that kind of thing
about themselves. That would be too complacent and self-
righteous.

We speak of the ancient race of Israel as God's chosen
people. Did God choose them because they deserved it?
Perhaps they sometimes thought He had, and that was when
they became most intolerably self-righteous. But the best
of them did not think so—and it is a remarkable thing how
their prophets used to tell them that God had not set His love
upon them because they were a very desirable or amiable or
worthy people, but out of His sheer spontaneous goodness
and grace. You know that mean little modern rhyme:

How odd
Of God
To choose
The Jews!

That is very meanly intended. But the sting is taken out of
it when you discover that the best of them quite acknowledged, and even pointed out, how odd it was of God to
choose them. God's true elect always see that. They know
that it is just like God to choose unlikely people. Paul asked:

183

'Hasn't God chosen the foolish and the weak and the base and even the nonentities?' And Paul thought it was strangest of all that God had chosen him. He was not fit to be called an apostle, he had even been a persecutor. But God in His sheer unmerited grace and love chose him and called him.

That is how Christ's people always speak of their election. And doesn't that throw a new light on the whole doctrine of Election?

(3) *God does not choose us to be His favourites, but to be His servants.* It is not like an oriental king choosing his favourites that he may give them a good time as his courtiers. It is more like a general choosing men for some daring and dangerous venture. That was a lesson that the Chosen People of Israel had to learn. At first they thought God had chosen them to be His pampered favourites. But they came to learn that He had chosen them to be His suffering servant. They were carried away into captivity in a strange land, and they learned that this was God's great purpose for them, that they should witness for Him in that strange land, and be a light to lighten the Gentiles, costly though that might be. And the same is true of all those great men whose names I mentioned in Old Testament story. When God chose them, He called them, each one, to do something for Him in the world, something hard and painful which needed to be done. When Christ called Andrew the fisherman, He said: 'Follow me, and I will make you a fisher of men.' A far more difficult task than fishing for fish, and with far greater dangers than all the storms on the Sea of Galilee. Tradition tells us that finally Andrew the Apostle suffered martyrdom for his faith, was put to death by crucifixion as his Master had been. That was what he was chosen for.

Now doesn't that make a great difference to the doctrine of Election? If the Church of Christ, to which most of us belong, is to be called God's chosen people, the new Israel of God, it is not because we are God's favourites, and it is not that we are better than other people, but that God in His grace has called us to be His servants and His witnesses in the world whatever it may cost us.

(4) That brings me to the fourth thing about Election. *When God chooses and calls us, we also have to make our choice.* And in one sense it all depends on that. God does not treat us as marionettes, manipulating us and saving us against our wills, for that would not be salvation at all. And again, God does not leave anybody out who really wants to come in. As a famous preacher once said: 'The elect are whosoever will, and the non-elect are whosoever won't.' 'Those whose names are written in the Lamb's book of life'—does that mean everybody? Does it include everybody? Yes, it includes everybody who really is willing to be included, everybody who hears Christ calling him by name, and *is willing to put down his name.*

Do you remember a splendid passage in the *Pilgrim's Progress* about one of the things that Christian saw in a vision in the Interpreter's house? He saw the door of a palace, and around it a crowd of people who wanted to go in but were afraid to do so. Outside the door there was a man sitting at a table, with a book and pen and ink, waiting to take down the names of any who would enter at the door. But in the doorway there stood a company of armed men to keep the door and to attack any who tried to enter.

'At last', says Bunyan, 'when every man started back for fear of the armed men, Christian saw a man of very stout countenance come up to the man that sat there to write, saying SET DOWN MY NAME, SIR. . . . Then Christian smiled, and said, I think verily I know the meaning of this.'

And so do we. God calls us to make our choice, to put down our names, and that is the final meaning of the doctrine of Election.

24. THE WORD AND THE BREAD

[Sermon preached before Holy Communion]

The cup of blessing which we bless, is it not the communion of the blood of Christ? The bread which we break, is it not the communion of the body of Christ?   1 CORINTHIANS 10.16

That which was from the beginning, which we have heard, which we have seen with our eyes, which we have looked upon, and our hands have handled, of the Word of life.   1 JOHN 1.1

IN many ways the Old Testament was a preparation for the New. The chosen people was being prepared by God to be the cradle of the Gospel of Christ. And one of the ways in which that preparation was going on was this: the chosen people, the people of Israel, were never allowed to use any kind of picture or image of God in their religion. Every schoolboy knows that one of their commandments said: 'Thou shalt not make unto thee any graven image or any likeness. . . .' That meant not merely that they must not worship idols, or have images of strange gods and bow down to them. Far more than that: they were not allowed to make any pictures or statues of Jehovah, their own true God. They must do without that in their worship.

I have no doubt the Israelites sometimes thought that was a very hard rule. It was very austere. It seemed to make worship so much more difficult. We do seem to need something visible, something tangible, something on which we can concentrate, to help our minds to realize the unseen God. We are creatures of flesh and blood—we seem to need such help. And all the other nations had it. The other races, round about Israel, had pictures and images of their gods. They could point and say: 'God is like that.' They could concentrate their gaze, and worship. Why couldn't the chosen people be allowed to have that kind of help too? It would make it so much easier to worship Jehovah.

But the prophets said: No. Jehovah the God of Israel will not have His people make pictures and images of Him. He is greater and more wonderful than any picture. How could any picture, or any image, really be like Him? And if they started using a picture or an image, it would only impoverish and degrade their thoughts of God. It would not really help their worship. In the long run, it would spoil their worship. So, if you had gone into the Temple in Jerusalem, you would have found that in that respect it was different from all the other temples in the world. You would have found great beauty and splendour of architecture, with plenty of religious symbolism, but no image of God. Even if you had been able to look into the Most Holy Place, the inner shrine where only the High Priest could go, you would have found no visible expression of the divine presence. The place was empty. There was no image of God. And in all the archaeological discoveries of recent years in Palestine, there has never yet been dug up any relic of what could be called an image of the Lord God of Israel.

The prophets gave the people 'the Word of God,' and that was enough. Words are safer than images. Words are a better guide in our worship. We must be content with the Word. 'Thou shalt not make unto thee any graven image.'

Now in what way was all that a good preparation for the Gospel? In this way. To those people of Israel, who had been kept to the hard rule of worshipping Him in words without graven images, God at last gave an image of Himself which was worth waiting for—something which their eyes could see and their hands could handle of the Word of life— Jesus Christ, God manifest in the flesh. Now they need no longer be content with mere words, even with the Word of

God. For now the Word has become flesh and dwelt among them and they can behold His glory—in Jesus Christ. Now God, who had kept them so long waiting, has found a way of giving them an 'image' of Himself that can really reveal Him, in a human life of flesh and blood—in Jesus Christ. Now His people can go far beyond what anyone had ever said before about God—they can do something far more startling than point to an image of God in a temple. They can point to a real Man, a living Man on earth, and say: 'God is like that. There is God Incarnate.' They can say to all the world: 'That which was from the beginning, which we have heard, which we have seen with our eyes, which we have looked upon, and our hands have handled, of the Word of life. For the life was manifested, and we have seen it.'

That is what we Christians always come back to, and always thank God for, as the great gift of the Gospel: that God has revealed Himself to us in Jesus Christ. The word 'God' is the most profound and mysterious word in all human speech. It stands for a great mystery. Anybody who has ever really tried to pray must have felt it. How can we pray to an infinite mysterious Being whom we can't see, whom no one has ever seen? How are we to conceive Him in our minds when we try to address Him? Our minds sometimes flounder helplessly, in thought and prayer: it is so hard to realize the presence of God. But then we remember that we are not left to ourselves. We remember God's great gift. We come back to the Gospel story, back to Jesus Christ. And as we see that human life of Jesus on the page of the Gospels, and on the soil of Palestine, then we know that we need not wonder and flounder any more. Seeing Jesus, we see the Father, and we know what God is like—the God and Father of our Lord Jesus Christ. So on this glad morning, in the fellowship of the Church, we can thank God with all our hearts for this: that He has given us an image of Himself to help our worship: Jesus Christ 'the Image of the Invisible God'.

But that is only the first stage. God has given us even something more, to meet our need, this morning. After all, we do need something more. It is nineteen centuries since Jesus lived on earth, when Peter and James and John saw Him with their eyes, and touched Him with their hands. The Word was made flesh, and they could touch that flesh. But we can't. Blessed indeed were the eyes that saw the things they saw. But these are not our eyes. God was incarnate in Jesus, but the Incarnate Life came to an end; and that was all 1900 years ago, and to us it is an old old story. A wonderful story, no doubt, but even the best of stories is made up of words. And must we then again be content with words—as if the Word had not become flesh? When we are weary of words, when we want something that our eyes can see and our hands can handle, has God nothing to give us, to help our weak minds to draw near to Him?

The answer to that question is *the Sacrament of the Lord's Supper*. The Gospel of the Incarnation would not be complete if it were not also the Gospel of the Sacraments. God in His mercy has given us something that we can see and touch and handle, to be a continuation for ever of the Incarnation. 'This bread which we break, is it not the communion of the body of Christ?' 'On the night on which He was betrayed, the Lord Jesus took bread, and when He had given thanks, He broke it, saying: "Take, eat, this is my body." ' The Word became flesh once for all; but in every age the Word becomes Sacrament, to help your weak faith and mine. Thank God for that.

Many a time Jesus, the Perfect Teacher, had taken some simple object-lesson to awaken the imagination of His disciples and to help their faith. Once He spoke of a costly pearl, to illustrate the incomparable worth of God's Kingdom. Once He spoke of a lamp, to illustrate how His disciples ought to shine in the world. Once He pointed to the lilies of the field, to illustrate God's providential care. And these were all parables. But finally, on the last night of His life, on the eve of His Cross, when the days of His flesh on earth were at an end, it was something much deeper He had to communicate to His disciples, something still more difficult. And the thing He took, to set before their eyes, was something much simpler and more universal. He did not take a pearl, or a lamp, or a lily. He took something much more ordinary, something which lay on the table before Him, something so common that it always is lying on the table before us—so that His disciples, anywhere in all the world, and in any age, however poor, can have it. The Lord Jesus took bread, and said 'Take, eat, this is my body'.

I'm sure His disciples didn't understand half of what it meant. But after He was gone, it came back to them, and they began to do it over again in His name. And whenever they did it, they felt and knew that after all Christ was not far away from them. Sometimes in their endeavour to live the Christian life they would grow weary and doubtful and dim-sighted, just as we do. Jesus seemed but a distant memory, an unreal shadow. But then they would come together, and do this simple thing. And the reality of Christ came back to them again. 'He became known unto them in the breaking of the bread.'

And so it has gone on ever since. And it sums up the whole Gospel, in something that we can see with our eyes and touch with our hands. The Sacrament of the Bread and the Wine sets before us all that Jesus was, all that Jesus did, all that God did through Him, the meaning of His coming, of His life, of His death, of His resurrection. 'God so loved the world, that He gave His only-begotten Son, that whoso-ever believeth on Him should not perish, but have eternal life.' 'God commendeth his love toward us in that while we were yet sinners Christ died for us.' 'To as many as received him, to them he gave the power to become children of God.' 'I believe in God the Father Almighty, Maker of heaven and earth; and in Jesus Christ his only Son our Lord.... I believe in the Holy Ghost, the holy Catholic Church, the Communion of Saints; the Forgiveness of sins; the Resurrection of the body, and the Life everlasting.' These are great words. That is the Word of the Gospel, and you know it all. It is what our whole Christian life is based on. But at the Table of Communion, the Word becomes Sacrament, that we in all the weakness of our faith may have something which we can see with our eyes and touch with our hands. Friends, it may be that some of us have come to Church today without much faith or hope or love. But God is waiting to be gracious to us, in the Sacrament of the Lord's Supper. As we celebrate it, may our faith be kindled to realize that the grace of the Lord Jesus Christ is as near and as real as the bread which we can see with our eyes and touch with our hands.

O God, who by the blood of Thy dear Son hast consecrated for us a new and living way into the holiest of all: grant us now, we beseech Thee, the assurance of Thy mercy, and sanctify us by Thy heavenly grace; that we, approaching Thee with pure heart and cleansed conscience, may offer unto Thee a sacrifice in righteousness, through Jesus Christ our Lord.

25. CHRIST WASHING THE DISCIPLES' FEET

[Sermon preached before Holy Communion]

Peter saith unto him, Thou shalt never wash my feet. Jesus answered him, If I wash thee not, thou hast no part with me. Simon Peter saith unto him, Lord, not my feet only, but also my hands and my head. Jesus saith to him, He that is washed needeth not save to wash his feet, but is clean every whit: and ye are clean, but not all.   JOHN 13.8-10

THERE are many puzzling things about St. John's Gospel, and some puzzling things about this particular story. It is a very curious thing that St. John tells us nothing at all of Jesus celebrating the Passover with His disciples on the last night of His life, as the other three Gospels do. And it is a still more curious thing that while the other three Gospels give us elaborate accounts of the instituting of the Lord's Supper on that last night of Jesus' life, St. John tells us nothing at all about it. He leaves out that story altogether, and instead he gives us on that last night a story of Jesus washing the feet of His disciples.

Now that is indeed very puzzling. Only we know that St. John's Gospel is in every way different from the others. St. John never seems to care very much about the exact facts, the mere outward happenings. He tells the story in his own mystical way, thinking more of the inward meaning than of the outward facts. And when you read his Gospel carefully, you come to realize that every line of it has hidden meanings which the casual eye does not catch. Certainly that is the case with this story. Every word of it almost seems to be scintillating with mystical meanings. The little bit that we have taken for our text is a conversation carried on between Simon Peter and Jesus, about the matter of the feet-washing. But we can't help seeing that it is much more. And as you read it, it is no longer simply an ancient conversation about feet-washing between Peter and Jesus, but in a timeless and mystical sense it is a dialogue between the soul of a Christian and its Lord, about some of the deepest realities of religion.

Moreover, though the celebration of the Lord's Supper is never mentioned at all, I believe it is not far away from the thoughts of the writer. And I think this little bit of conversation, when we read between the lines, provides some thoughts very suitable to us as we go forward to our celebration. Let us take it in four stages.

(1) *Peter speaks.* '*Lord, thou shalt never wash my feet.*' On the surface that is simply the natural shrinking of a disciple from having this menial service performed for him by his Master. But when you go deeper, it becomes the humble shrinking which any Christian may feel from the gifts and influences and sacraments of the Christian religion. Or, in other words, the sense of unworthiness.

It would seem that from the very earliest times the Sacrament of the Lord's Supper used to raise in the minds of Christians this question of 'worthy or unworthy?' For St. Paul speaks of it. According to him there is such a thing as eating this bread and drinking this cup unworthily, and so he tells us that we ought to examine ourselves. And thus ever since then the thought of this Sacrament has been accustomed to bow down Christian men and women in humility, penitence, and confession, with a sense of unworthiness.

Well, I want to begin by suggesting that that is a good and wholesome thing. 'Lord,' cries Simon Peter, 'thou shalt never wash my feet,' and we think more of him in the story for saying that and for feeling it. It sounds so healthy and natural and right when we read it in the story. And in its spiritual sense as applied to ourselves, when we think of the privileges of the Gospel, it is natural and right and healthy too.

The trouble with us often is that we are far too complacent about these things. Instead of humbly remembering our own shortcomings we dwell upon the faults of our neighbours, we think of their unworthiness. Yes, I believe sometimes even at the Lord's Table we do that. We look round uncharitably, we tell ourselves that this man is not a very good Christian, or we ask in our hearts what right that man has to be there; when we ought rather to be asking what right we have to be there ourselves. When that spirit is in us, of pointing out other people's sins, it is a pretty good proof that we are not humbly penitent for our own. We are complacent. We approach the mysteries of religion quite lightly, as if religion were a little and ordinary thing to be taken for granted, as if there were no wonderful condescending unmerited love and grace in Christ's Gospel. It is as if Simon Peter, in the story, should complacently accept the foot-washing from Jesus without a thought. And we accept the Sacrament in that spirit too. And when we do accept religion and the Sacrament in that spirit, as a little ordinary commonplace thing, then of course it becomes a little thing, and it doesn't do us much good, and we don't grow in grace, our hearts don't grow in strength and purity and love and courage, our hearts remain just as they were, because we are not humble enough for the grace of God.

And therefore, don't you see what a healthy thing it would be for us at a time like this, and at any time, to become humbly steadily conscious of our faults of character, our unworthiness? 'Lord,' says Simon Peter, 'thou shalt never wash my feet.'

(2) *Jesus speaks: 'If I wash thee not, thou hast no part with me,'* which means, I suppose, that the sense of unworthiness, even though it is wholesome, must never keep us from accepting God's grace. You see Jesus corrects Peter, puts

him right. It is good to feel unworthy, but there is a danger
in it when it holds the soul back from entering on its true
heritage. And there is a kind of false humility which instead
of opening the soul to God's grace rather shuts up the soul
in its own misery.

It takes various forms. For instance, some people spoil
the Sacrament of the Lord's Supper for themselves by being
afraid of it, by shrinking from it, by thinking gloomy
thoughts about it. Instead of making it a joyful helpful
thing, an hour of banquet and of song, they look upon it
with a superstitious terror, or a doubtful shrinking, and go
through it in such a way that they are glad when it is over.
Then of course it does not give them fellowship with Christ
or help them much at all. And again, many of us go through
it in a half-hearted unexpectant unaspiring way, not wishing
to be very much influenced by it. Indeed we are too apt to
do that with our religion all over. We don't want to go
very far with it. It may be that we do not want to be very
thoroughly cleansed from our sins, searched out by the Holy
Spirit of God and separated from all that is evil; we are not
prepared for that sacrifice. But to such a spirit came those
words: 'If I wash thee not, thou hast no part with me.'

Or it may be again that with a false humility we tell
ourselves that the deepest things of religion are not for the
like of us. I think many would-be Christians are apt to do
that: to go in for a superficial conventional kind of Christianity, without ever really venturing to claim for themselves
in the secret of their hearts the real superlative gifts of the
Christian Gospel. They assume in an unbelieving kind of
way that that is beyond them. They are like those unbelieving Israelites who, as they peeped into the promised
land, said 'We be not able to go up and conquer it'. And
that is throughout the Bible taken as the supreme sad example
of people who 'could not enter in because of unbelief',

people who were prevented from entering into their spiritual heritage by a false humility which was not the true childlike heart, but rather a hard proud heart of unbelief, shrinking back, and so frustrating the grace of God. Well, Christians do it still. They decide, unconsciously perhaps, to leave the really personal experiences of religion to other people who are more suited for that kind of thing, and for themselves to be content with something more humdrum and conventional. But oh, that is a mournful mistake, a mistake which makes religion really a most unhelpful burden, and leaves the heart weary and soiled when it might have a fountain of courage and cheer and cleansing. 'Thou shalt never wash my feet,' the foolish heart sometimes cries out, with a false humility and shrinking. And then comes this answer (and can't you see the spiritual meaning shimmering through the words?), 'If I wash thee not, thou hast no part with me'.

(3) *Peter speaks again: 'Lord, not my feet only, but also my hands and my head.'* It is not very difficult (is it?) to find the inner meaning this time. This is full eager confident acceptance and surrender. The disciple had felt a natural sense of unworthiness, and it had made him shrink back too much. But now that Christ has corrected him, he turns again to the ministrations of Christ, as humble as ever, but now eager and confident and trustful. Before he shrank back because of his unworthiness; but now, just because of his unworthiness, because of his need, he stretches out his hands for that help without which he is helpless indeed:

> Nothing in my hand I bring,
> Simply to Thy Cross I cling:
> Foul I to the fountain fly,
> Wash me, Saviour, or I die.

But then also something of this:

> Take my life and let it be
> Consecrated, Lord, to Thee . . .

196

Take my hands, and let them move
At the impulse of Thy love.
Take my feet, and let them be
Swift and beautiful for Thee . . .
Take myself, and I will be
Ever, only, all for Thee.

There is yearning and eagerness, whole-hearted aspiration and dedication: 'Lord, not my feet only, but also my hands and my head.'

There are times when that spirit springs up powerfully in the heart of a Christian man or woman. Through many of the days of our lives we Christian men and women are pretty unaspiring. We haven't much of the heavenly vision, we let it fade away and come to be content with a very mediocre Christian life. The world has its claims, and we become preoccupied with them; and our neighbours may be difficult, and we become loveless towards them; and our devotions sometimes seem a waste of time, and we become slack about them. And so the days run on, and we are living on a pretty commonplace level, though perhaps we hardly know it, with only half our hearts in the service of Christ. And then suddenly perhaps (it sometimes happens at a Communion season) we get a glimpse of the poor lives we are living, and we also get a glimpse of the beauty of holiness, the glory of a real genuine whole-hearted Christian life. Yes, and lest we should be discouraged, we at the same time get a glimpse of the wonderful infinite love of God in Jesus Christ, and His power to help us, and His high purpose for us, that we should be perfect as He is perfect. Then we are fired with holy enthusiasm and aspiration. We resolve in our hearts that henceforth we will not go back nor turn from God at all. Our hearts leap out in faith to God, cast themselves upon His grace, consecrate themselves to His will, dedicate themselves to His service. Our whole hearts go out to Christ our Master. They were indeed His already, but we remember it now in a fresh moment of self-dedication: 'Lord, not my feet only, but also my hands and my head.'

(4) *Jesus speaks again.* '*He that is washed needeth not save to wash his feet.*' Here again Jesus seems to be correcting Peter, in his over-impulsiveness. But can we again find a mystical meaning? Well, I can't help thinking of the Sacrament of the Lord's Supper, coming here and there on the Christian's pilgrimage, like a rest-house where the pilgrim may have the stains of travel washed from his feet. That is all he needs. Simon Peter is already a true disciple, he doesn't need to begin all over again, he is one of the clean ones; but he needs time and again, as a pilgrim, to have his feet washed. Well, all who sit down at the Lord's Table are professing to be true disciples. 'Ye are clean', says Christ to His true disciples. They are in a sense dedicated already. It does not have to be done all over again at every solemn season. And there is not much good in those emotional upheavals which leave us just as we were, and come again and again and find us and leave us no better. That is not what we have to seek and that is not what we depend on. What matters is the dedication of the will in faith and loyalty to God. And that is what we profess to have made and to be continuing every day in our pilgrimage, with the Slough of Sin left behind and our faces set towards Jerusalem. Yes, but even then, and however advanced in the Christian life we may be, there is the dust of the road, the sins that so easily beset us, leaving upon our feet the stains of travel. But every now and again we come to a pilgrims' hospice by the roadside, where the stains can be washed from our feet. That is done, of course, in our daily devotions and in our weekly worship. But the roadside hospices are especially the Sacramental seasons, bringing to us the assurance of the forgiveness of sins, bringing to us also spiritual cleansing and refreshment, and sending us forth

again ready for the journey. 'He that is washed needeth not save to wash his feet.'

Friends, you and I all profess to be pilgrims on the road. And now we have arrived at another Sacramental season. As we look back over the way we have travelled since our last one, and as we look at ourselves, must we not confess that much of the dust of the road had clung to us, yes and even of the mire that those pilgrims find who wander off the road? Our lives have not had in them much to show whose we are and whom we serve. There has been too much vanity and worldliness and lovelessness and uncharitableness and evil temper. And the stains of these things are upon us, though we profess the name of Christ. But here is the Pilgrim's Hospice, where we can be cleansed from these travel-stains, bathed in the mercy and love and grace of God.

O may we be able to approach our Sacrament as we ought: humble, but confident; not thinking of our neighbours' faults, but of our own; not even thinking too much of our own faults, but of the grace of God in Jesus Christ, which can forgive and cleanse and renew us, and send us upon our way rejoicing.

DATE DUE

MAR 5 '64	DEC 1 '70		
Soph 1	NOV 2 '77		
OCT 30 '64	AUG 2 '79		
JAN 21 '65			
FEB 18 '66	OCT 30 '85		
June 27			
JAN 8 '67			
JUN 2 '67			
Faculty			
1/4/68			
JAN 12 '68			
2/9/68			
2/26/68			
SEP 12 '68			
OCT 3 '68			
FEB 28 '69			
JAN 14 '70			
FEB 8 '70			